HENRY II

GREAT SEAL OF HENRY AS KING
(Obverse ½)

HENRY II

BY

L. F. SALZMAN B.A. F.S.A.

ILLUSTRATED

NEW YORK

Russell & Russell

FIRST PUBLISHED IN 1914
REISSUED, 1967, BY RUSSELL & RUSSELL
A DIVISION OF ATHENEUM HOUSE, INC.
BY ARRANGEMENT WITH L. F. SALZMAN
L. C. CATALOG CARD NO: 66-27144
PRINTED IN THE UNITED STATES OF AMERICA

CONTENTS

APPENDIX

ILLUSTRATIONS

HENRY II

CHAPTER I

HENRY FITZ-EMPRESS

WHEN the *White Ship* went down on 25th November 1120, carrying with her the only legitimate son of Henry I., the succession to the English throne became a question of great moment. Henry's daughter, Maud, had been married to Henry V., Emperor of Germany, in 1114; it was clearly impossible for England and Normandy to be ruled in conjunction with the Empire, and Maud had no children to whom her father's crown might pass. The king's unruly brother, Robert of Normandy, was still alive, but a prisoner in England; and his son William, the most formidable candidate for the throne, was destined to die in Flanders in 1128. But before death had removed this dangerous and unpopular competitor, a fresh solution of the difficulty had become possible. Maud's husband, the emperor, had died in 1125,[1] and on 1st January 1127,

[1] Later writers, anxious to depreciate Henry II. even to the extent of making him illegitimate, and his mother a bigamist, retailed a legend to the effect that the Emperor Henry V. had not died at this time, but had retired secretly into a monastery: Giraldus Cambrensis, *Op.* viii. 300.

A

King Henry declared Maud his heir, and caused the peers to swear to accept her as his successor in England and in Normandy. There was no precedent for female sovereignty in either country, and it was probably not anticipated that she should reign alone, but rather that she should by marriage bestow the crown upon some fitting partner. The important matter of this marriage Henry had virtually undertaken to submit to the decision of his barons, but at the end of May 1127 he betrothed her, with an absence of preparation that amounted almost to secrecy, to Geoffrey, son of Count Fulk of Anjou, a boy of fourteen, eleven years the junior of his bride. The marriage, as Henry had foreseen, was unpopular, though the addition of the neighbouring provinces of Anjou and Maine to Normandy made the King of England the most powerful of all the feudatories of France.

The marriage of Geoffrey, now Count of Anjou, and Maud took place in June 1129, but within a few weeks the quick-tempered count and his haughty bride had quarrelled and separated, and it was not until the autumn of 1131 that they came together again. Their reunion was made by Henry the occasion for causing his barons to renew their oath of allegiance to Maud as his successor, thereby quashing any objection that might have been made to the previous oath as invalidated by her marriage. The king was now more than sixty years old, and his anxiety for the future of his country and his dynasty

must have been greatly relieved by the birth of a son
to Geoffrey and Maud on the 25th March 1133.   The
boy was called Henry, after his grandfather, and it
is significant of the predominance attaching to his
mother, as heiress of England and Normandy, that
the title by which he was most commonly known to
his contemporaries was that of Henry Fitz-Empress.

The death of Henry I., on 1st December 1135,
seems to have taken the empress and her partisans
by surprise.   She went almost at once into Normandy
to press her claims, half-heartedly and with little
success; but in the meanwhile her cousin, Stephen of
Blois, nephew of the late king, had crossed into
England, and, with the assistance of his brother,
Henry, Bishop of Winchester, had caused himself to
be crowned king on 22nd December.   The Norman
barons accepted Stephen, and the final blow was given
to Maud's cause by the Pope's declaration in favour
of her rival.   Her half-brother, however, Earl Robert
of Gloucester, was not long in forming a party to support the claims of Maud and her son in England,
and in 1139 Maud herself crossed the Channel with a
small body of troops.   With the varying fortunes of
the long-continued war between the empress and
Stephen we are not concerned, but it was when
Maud's cause was almost at its worst, in the winter
of 1142, that her young son Henry, then in his tenth
year, came over in charge of his uncle, Earl Robert,
and was settled at Bristol.   There he remained for
four years under the tuition of a certain Master

Matthew, who cultivated in him that love for learning which made him in later days the most literary prince of his time and a worthy successor of his scholarly grandfather.

During those four years Henry's father, Geoffrey of Anjou, had been strengthening his position on the Continent, though apparently making no effort to assist his wife in her struggle with Stephen. By the end of 1143 he had secured control of the greater part of Normandy, and early in 1144 Rouen surrendered and Geoffrey was recognised as Duke of Normandy. Having established himself securely he now sent for his son to join him, and accordingly, late in 1146, or at the beginning of the next year, Earl Robert of Gloucester escorted young Henry to Wareham and there bade farewell to him. Uncle and nephew were destined to meet no more, for on 31st October 1147 Earl Robert died. Immediately the earl's death was known, Earl Gilbert of Pembroke, whose castle of Pevensey was then undergoing a siege, urged Henry's return. He considered that the only hope for the empress's cause, now that its mainstay had departed, lay in the presence of Henry in England. The boy—he was only fourteen—hurriedly crossed with a few companions, landed at one of the western ports, and made feeble attacks on Cricklade and Bourton, in Gloucestershire, from which he was easily driven off. His forces dwindled rather than increased, and his scanty supply of money soon came to an end. An application to

his mother for further funds proved ineffectual, as
she was in the same straits herself. He then turned
to the Earl of Gloucester for assistance ; but Earl
William was very different from his father; he cared
little for war, had no enthusiasm for the cause of
his cousin, and saw no reason why he should waste
his treasure on a desperate and hopeless enterprise.
Unable for lack of funds either to continue his in-
judicious venture or to leave the country, the
humiliated prince had to apply for help to the rival
whom he had so rashly attacked. Stephen, always
chivalrous and good-natured even to weakness, in
spite of the opposition and remonstrances of his
advisers, at once supplied Henry with the necessary
means of returning to his father's court, where, in
the early spring of 1148, he was joined by his mother,
the empress.[1]

Geoffrey, now that he was firmly established in
Normandy, seems to have begun to plan the

[1] Mr. Round (*Feudal England*, 491–4) rejects the "Invasion of
1147," of which the only mention is the account given in the *Gesta
Stephani*, and considers that the events recorded relate to Henry's
visit in 1149. He is undoubtedly right in pointing out that the
chronicler confused Henry's unwarlike cousin, Earl William of Gloucester, with his loyal uncle, Earl Robert, making the latter refuse to
give that help which, had he then been living, he would certainly have
rendered to the utmost of his ability. On the other hand, what we
know of Henry's visit to England in 1149 is quite inconsistent with
the wretched fiasco described in the *Gesta*, and when Mr. Round argues
that " the statement that Henry applied for help to his mother by no
means involves . . . her presence in England at the time," it is
difficult to follow his argument. Had Henry applied for money
to any one outside England it would presumably have been to his
father, and, moreover, in 1149 the empress could not have been in
straitened circumstances.

aggrandisement of his son, in whose right he had obtained the duchy. And so, in April 1149, Henry was sent to England to receive the honour of knighthood from King David of Scotland, his mother's uncle. Landing, probably, at Wareham, he made a brief stay at Devizes, where we find in his company Roger, Earl of Hereford, Patrick, Earl of Salisbury, William Beauchamp, John St. John, Roger Berkeley, Hubert de Vaux, Henry Hussey, Manser Bisset and others.[1] Thence he passed peacefully northwards, the whole of western England being in the hands of magnates, such as the Earls of Leicester and Warwick, who were friendly to his cause or at least hostile to that of Stephen. To Carlisle he was brought by Earl Ralph of Chester, and there he was received by King David and his son Henry, Earl of Northumberland, and on Whitsunday, 22nd May, was duly invested with the insignia of knighthood. Henry and his ally of Scotland now persuaded the powerful Earl of Chester to join forces with them against Stephen, but before this scheme could be carried out King Stephen had outbid his rivals and bought the support of the earl by a bestowal of fiefs so lavish as to render him almost king of northern England.

Returning to his father in January 1150, Henry was invested with the dukedom of Normandy. But a little more than a year later Stephen's son, Eustace, persuaded King Louis of France, with whom Geoffrey

---

[1] See list of witnesses to charter executed at Devizes on 13th April, 1149 : *Sarum Charters* (Rolls Ser.), 16.

(1)

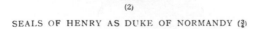

(2)

SEALS OF HENRY AS DUKE OF NORMANDY (⅔)

had quarrelled, to assist him in regaining Normandy.
The allies advanced as far as Arques, where they were
opposed by the forces under the young duke. Henry
here exhibited that scrupulous respect for his feudal
overlord, the King of France, which he displayed
so conspicuously in later years, and acted on the
defensive, refusing to attack his suzerain. Eustace
was a man of warlike spirit, but King Louis, who,
though not averse to war, seems to have had a profound distaste for fighting, did not care to risk a
battle and retired for the time. Later in the year he
despatched another force to operate against Mantes,
but Geoffrey now came to terms and agreed to surrender the Vexin, the borderland between France
and Normandy, on condition that Louis should
confirm Henry in the possession of the rest of the
Norman duchy, and these terms the French king
gladly accepted.

Henry had now established his claim to half of
his grandfather's dominions, and began to plan the
recovery of the remainder by an invasion of England.
His plans, however, were interfered with by the
sudden death of his father on 7th September 1151.
The recovery of England was postponed, but a
great accession of territory was obtained by Henry
in the following spring. Louis VII. had married
Eleanor, the heiress of Aquitaine, in 1137, but
relations between the able and energetic queen and
her feeble husband had gradually become strained to
breaking, and at last, early in 1152, they discovered

that they ought never to have married, being related
to one another, distantly but within the degrees
theoretically prohibited by the Church.[1] A divorce
was granted on 18th March, and Eleanor, avoiding
the too pressing attentions of Count Theobald of
Blois and Geoffrey of Anjou, Henry's younger
brother, intimated her willingness to bestow her
hand and great possessions upon the Duke of Normandy. Henry, now nineteen, but with a reputation that many an older man might have envied,
hastened at once to meet Eleanor at Poitiers, and
they were married in May. By this marriage Henry
became master of Aquitaine and Poitou, in addition
to Anjou, Maine, and Normandy, and his rule reached
from the Channel to the Pyrenees.

He now once more prepared for the invasion of
England, and was assembling his forces at Barfleur
in June when he found himself called upon to face
the combined forces of Eleanor's late husband, King
Louis, and her disappointed suitors, Count Theobald
and Geoffrey of Anjou. Henry displayed the energy
and rapidity of movement which in later years made
the French king declare that he must be able to fly,
dashed down to Pacey and prepared to attack the
French forces, but Louis, with his usual discretion,
retired at once. Henry promptly turned north to
crush the rebellious Richer of L'Aigle and destroy
his robbers' castle of Bonmoulins. The Norman

---

[1] The connection between Louis and Eleanor was very distant, but
a literal observance of the Canon Law would have invalidated the
marriages of half the nobility of Europe.

frontier had been secured before the end of August, and the duke was free to turn his hand against his brother Geoffrey, which he did very effectually, reducing Montsoreau and compelling Geoffrey to sue for peace. A truce patched up between Henry and Louis was speedily renounced by the latter, but Henry, estimating his adversary's military abilities at a low rate, continued his preparations for the invasion of England, and eventually crossed about the second week in January 1153, with a fleet of thirty-six ships.

It was probably at Wareham that Henry landed with his hundred and forty men-at-arms and three thousand infantry, and he would seem to have gone straight to Bristol, where he was joined by those magnates who had supported his cause in the past, or who considered that it would be to their advantage to do so in the future. Operations were at once begun against Malmesbury Castle, and the outer works were speedily carried, but the massive keep was too strong to be stormed and could only be reduced by starvation. Meanwhile Stephen had collected his forces and was marching to the rescue ; after halting for the night at Cirencester he advanced to the relief of Malmesbury, but found the little Avon swollen and impassable, while a bitter wind and blinding rain and sleet, driving in the faces of his men, made it impossible for him to advance or to retain his position. Abandoning his enterprise, the king marched back to London, and the castellan

Jordan had no choice but to surrender. Enheartened
by the capture of Malmesbury, Henry now directed
his energies to the particular business which had
brought him over—the relief of Wallingford. During
the past five or six years, although the country as
a whole had been at peace, some of the more restless spirits had carried on a sort of war on their own
account, and of these one of the most prominent had
been Brian Fitz-Count of Wallingford. In 1152 he
had managed to destroy the castles set up at Bright-
well and Reading to keep him in check, and Stephen
had been obliged to besiege Wallingford Castle and
blockade it by the erection of counter-works at
Crowmarsh. Finding themselves in difficulties, the
garrison had sent over to Henry for assistance, and
he now came to the rescue and invested Crowmarsh.
An outlying portion of the royalist siege works on
Wallingford Bridge had already fallen into his
hands, when Stephen once more offered fight. Henry,
for his part, was very willing to give battle and drew
out his forces, but the desire of the prelates to avoid
further bloodshed, and the fear of the barons that a
decisive victory might destroy the balance of power
between the two parties and so render their own
services less marketable, resulted in secret negotiations, and compelled the rivals to agree to a truce
for five days, though suggestions for a more permanent
cessation of hostilities, made at a private interview
between Henry and Stephen, came to nothing. The
terms of the truce were highly favourable to Henry,

the king being obliged to withdraw his garrison from
Crowmarsh and allow the fortifications to be dismantled.

Wallingford having been relieved, and the royalists
under William Cheyney and Richard de Lucy having
been defeated in a cavalry action near Oxford,
Henry seems to have recruited his forces in the
western counties, visiting Evesham and Warwick,
where the Countess Gundreda handed over to him
the castle, from which she had ejected Stephen's
garrison. Then, turning eastwards, he besieged and
captured Stamford Castle about the same time that
Stephen reduced Ipswich. The duke next plundered
Nottingham, but did not attempt to take the castle
By this time the peace party were beginning to
gain the upper hand, and the efforts of Archbishop
Theobald and Bishop Henry of Winchester gained
strength by the removal of their chief opponent,
the king's son, Eustace of Boulogne. That bellicose
ruffian, enraged at the tame conclusion of the
Wallingford affair, had gone off on a ravaging
expedition in the eastern counties. After plundering Cambridgeshire he paid a similar attention to
the lands of Bury St. Edmunds, rashly pillaging
the monastic lands on St. Laurence's Day (10th
August). The offended saints were not slow to
avenge the outrage, and within a week Eustace
lay dead. With his death died Stephen's hopes of
founding a dynasty, for his younger son, William,
had borne no part in the civil war and possessed

neither the desire nor the ability to contest the crown
with Henry.

After some weeks of negotiation a compromise
was at last arrived at by which Stephen was to retain
the crown for life on condition of acknowledging
Henry as his heir, and on 6th November 1153 this
agreement was ratified by the peers in council at
Winchester; the rivals were reconciled and the barons
of both parties did homage to the king and his successor. From Winchester the double court moved
to London, where the news of the termination of the
long and ruinous struggle was received with the
greatest enthusiasm; and after Christmas king and
duke met once more, at Oxford, on 13th January
1154, just a year since Henry had landed in England.
A little later, when they met again, at Dunstable,
Henry reproached Stephen for not having fulfilled
one of the conditions of the treaty of peace, which
was that the castles built since the death of Henry I.
should be destroyed. The task was no small one,
as these so-called adulterine castles had sprung up
all over the country and were estimated by Robert
of Torigny, usually an accurate authority, to number
eleven hundred and fifteen. Stephen resented the
charge of ill-faith, but the quarrel, if it deserve the
name, was soon made up, and the two princes went
down to Dover together in February to meet the
Count and Countess of Flanders. While there it is
said that Stephen's Flemish mercenaries, without
his knowledge but with the connivance of his son

William, planned to murder Henry. Whether a
rumour of the plot reached his ears or whether he
considered that affairs in Normandy required his
presence, Henry soon afterwards parted from the
king and returned to Normandy, where he spent the
next five months strengthening his position. With
King Louis he was now on good terms; and he was
actually engaged in a military expedition on that
king's behalf when the throne of England fell to
him by the death of Stephen on 25th October 1154.

CHAPTER II

HENRY ascended the throne of England in singularly favourable circumstances. Still young, his character had been formed and his reputation had been established on the battle-fields of England and Normandy. Far inferior to his predecessor in personal character, he was as far his superior in kingcraft, possessing just those talents necessary for his position which the chivalrous, kindly, and erratic Stephen lacked. Something of this, which was to be demonstrated by the history of his reign, was already obvious, and the bulk of his English subjects were strongly prepossessed in his favour. The Church was on his side; the greater barons cared little who was king so long as their titles and their revenues were assured to them; the lesser lords and the peasantry, exhausted and impoverished by the twenty years of anarchy, welcomed a ruler strong enough to curb the lawless feuds of semi-independent chieftains, while, above all, there was no other claimant to the throne, the only possible rival, Stephen's son, William, Earl of Warenne and Surrey, being, fortunately for himself, quite unambitious of regal honours. Possessing great powers of physical endurance, Henry was as active

GREAT SEAL OF HENRY AS KING
(Reverse ⅓)

in mind as in body, a well-read scholar and an accomplished linguist ; short, sturdy, with coarse hands and freckled face, unkempt and careless in his dress, he overcame the disadvantages of an unattractive appearance by his courtesy and the charm of his manner, which made him formidable in diplomacy or love. Although inheriting the volcanic temper of his Angevin forefathers and liable to outbursts of diabolic rage, he ruled his hot blood with a cool head, practically never allowing his feelings to dictate his policy and but rarely indulging in acts of cruelty or revenge. He was non-religious rather than irreligious, non-moral rather than immoral ; though he made no attempt to bridle his lust, there is no reason to suppose that any of his numerous mistresses were unwilling victims ; and though his irreverence and contempt of the Church's sacraments shocked his contemporaries, he admired and chose for his friends such men as St. Hugh of Lincoln. Clear-sighted and self-centred, Henry was emphatically a strong man ; and it is the irony of fate that the weak spot which was to prove his ruin lay in his most unselfish and amiable trait, his affection for his family.

Not the least of Henry's qualifications for the kingship was his ability to select the right men for his ministers. It is possible that Archbishop Theobald may have had some influence in the appointment of the brilliant young Archdeacon of Canterbury, Thomas Becket, to the high office of Chancellor, but the king may be given the credit for choosing Robert,

Earl of Leicester, and Richard of Lucy as Justiciars. All three appointments proved to have been well made, and the first two were probably made before the coronation.[1] At this ceremony, on 19th December, besides the Archbishop of Canterbury, to whose see belonged the privilege of crowning the king, there were present the Archbishops of York and of Rouen, fourteen English bishops and the bishops of Bayeux, Lisieux, and Avranches, numbers of foreign noblemen, including Dietrich, Count of Flanders, and a multitude of English and Norman lords. There were the king's two brothers—Geoffrey, with whom he was shortly to be at war for the second time, and William, for whose benefit he was no doubt already planning the conquest of Ireland ; there were the royal officers Henry of Essex, Constable of England, Richard de Humet, Constable of Normandy, Warin Fitz-Gerald, the Chamberlain, and Hugh, Earl of Norfolk, hereditary High Steward ; and there amongst the brilliant crowd would be such great lords as Reynold, Earl of Cornwall, son of King Henry I., and William, Earl of Arundel, the confirmation of whose privileges and estates was one of the new king's first acts. Abbots, royal chaplains, clerks of the Chancery and Exchequer, wealthy merchants and burgesses, and the ladies of the court with their attendants, whose gay robes formed but the highest tone in an assembly

---

[1] It is not quite certain when Richard de Luci was associated with the Earl of Leicester in the justiciarship, but the earl was clearly Chief Justiciar until his death in 1168, and may have held the superior position by priority of appointment.

blazing with colour, complete the picture. Yet of all those in whose presence Henry swore to follow in the footsteps of his grandfather, to maintain the good laws of the realm and to abate the bad, very few were English and few even spoke the English tongue. The governing classes in Church and State were Norman by lineage, language, and sympathy, and at a time when an Englishman sat in St. Peter's chair [1] scarce any of his compatriots held offices of trust in their native country. The fusion of English and Norman, which had already spread so far in the lower ranks of society, only began to affect the higher ranks in the course of the reign of Henry, who, by the ultimate failure of his life-long policy, was to give the English nation its individuality.

The affairs of the kingdom could not be neglected for coronation festivities, and at his Christmas court, held at Bermondsey, Henry took the first step for ensuring peace by the expulsion of the lawless Flemish mercenaries. Their leader, William of Ipres, was allowed to retain the large revenues from lands in Kent granted to him by Stephen and well earned by his loyalty and skill, and some few of his followers were sent to join the colony of Flemings established on the borders of Wales, but the bulk of the " Flemish wolves " were packed off to satisfy their appetite for war and plunder on the Continent. Having thus disposed of these alien robbers, the king had next

---

[1] Nicholas Brakespere, the only Englishman to attain the papacy, was elected pope and took the title of Adrian IV. in December 1154.

to deal with those of his own subjects who had abused their own powers and the weakness of the central government during the anarchy to extend their possessions at the expense of the royal demesnes and to strengthen their position by the erection of castles. The destruction of the " adulterine " castles, erected without royal licence, had been promised, and to some extent performed, by Stephen in the last months of his reign,[1] but Henry now determined to complete the work and at the same time to revoke the grants of royal demesne whether made by King Stephen or by the empress.

In thus recovering the Crown lands the king was no doubt partly influenced by the desire to increase the very scanty royal revenues, and partly by his deliberate anti-feudal policy. It did not require the acute intelligence which Henry possessed to learn from the events of the last twenty years that it would be wise to clip the wings of the great barons, who threatened to overshadow the throne itself, and to play for popular support. It was clearly to his interest that the people should be prosperous, contented, and loyal, and he was not slow to adopt measures which would render the nobles less able alike to oppose the Crown and to oppress the people. Throughout his reign he acted on these anti-feudal principles. Although Henry had a distinct appreciation of justice, it may be doubted if the legal

---

[1] Roger of Hoveden mentions in particular the Yorkshire castle of Drax as one of the last of many destroyed by Stephen.

reforms, which were in many ways the most important features of his reign, would ever have seen the light had they not tended towards the elevation of the smaller men and the consequent depression of the greater. With a few exceptions it will be found that when Henry required, as he usually did, to increase his revenues by means of doubtful legality, he preferred to extort large sums from the wealthy rather than an equivalent multitude of small amounts from the poorer classes. So also the frequent substitution of money payments for military service helped to discourage the maintenance of large bands of armed retainers, kept nominally for the king's service but liable to be used for the furthering of their lord's ambition. Yet in all cases Henry acted with a wise moderation, which, leaving the great lords in possession of their titles and estates, left them in the position of having more to lose than gain by rebellion.

The king's orders were as a whole acquiesced in with little resistance, the estates wrested from the Crown were restored, the castles demolished, life and property were once more secure, commerce revived, the merchants came forth to find customers and the Jews to seek their debtors. But William of Aumâle, Earl of Yorkshire, who, under Stephen, had enjoyed a semi-regal independence, hesitated to conform to the new state of affairs, and prepared to offer armed resistance to the king's demands. Henry left Oxford, whither he had gone at the beginning of the new year, 1155, and moved slowly northwards, halting appa-

rently at Northampton to re-create Hugh Bigot, Earl
of Norfolk, his charter taking the form of a re-creation
rather than a confirmation, possibly as a hint to the
shifty earl that his dignities were not secure beyond
all risk. By the time that the king reached York
Earl William, finding himself unsupported, had recon-
sidered his position and wisely submitted to the royal
demands, surrendering his fortress of Scarborough.
A precipitous bluff projecting into the sea, whose
waves washed it on three sides, joined to the main-
land only on the west by a narrow neck, the rock
of Scarborough presented an ideal spot for the rear-
ing of a castle, and here accordingly the earl had
set his great stronghold, surrounding the spacious
plateau on the top of the cliff with a wall, digging a
well, and building a keep four-square upon the narrow
neck by which alone access was possible. Nestling
against the western base of the rock lay the little
town of Scarborough, itself surrounded with a wall
and thus forming an outwork of the castle. The
position was too formidable to be left in the hands
of a subject, and King Henry took care to retain it
for the remainder of his reign; and when in the course
of a few years the earl's keep fell into decay, it was
rebuilt and enlarged at a cost equivalent to some
£10,000 of modern money, the work beginning in 1159
and spreading over the next three years.[1]

[1] After his description of Earl William's great castle of Scarborough, William de Neuburgh adds that when in course of time it
fell into decay, King Henry rebuilt it. It is rather surprising to find
how soon this occurred, but the Pipe Roll for 1159 shows £111 spent

On his way either to or from York Henry appears
to have visited Lincoln, the priory of Spalding, and
the great abbeys of Peterborough, Thorney, and
Ramsey.　The news of the king's approach to
Nottingham so stirred the guilty conscience of
William Peverel, burdened with the murder of the
Earl of Chester, that he sought to save body and
soul at the expense of his possessions by becoming
a monk in a priory of which he was himself patron
at Lenton.　It was no doubt while in the neighbour-
hood of Nottingham that the king received information of the birth of his second son, Henry, on
28th February, and shortly afterwards he returned
to London, where he held a council at the end of
March.　During the previous three months Roger,
Earl of Hereford, had been contemplating resistance
to the king's demands for the surrender of his castles,
but the arguments of his kinsman, Gilbert Foliot,
Bishop of Hereford, supported by the success of
Henry's expedition into Yorkshire, brought him to
a wiser mind, and he placed the castles of Hereford
and Gloucester in the king's hands.　Hugh de
Mortimer, however, the great lord of the Welsh
Marches, who had been the chief instigator of Earl
Roger's disaffection, maintained his attitude of opposition and fortified his castles of Cleobury, Wigmore,

---

" on the works of the castle of Scardeburc," and £70 spent on the
works of the " tower " (*turris*), a term which Mr. Round has shown
to imply a keep.　Next year £94, 3s. 4d. was spent on the keep, and
the following year £107, 6s. 8d. on the castle.

and Bridgnorth. Henry accordingly moved west,
halting at Wallingford, where on 10th April he held a
council at which the nobles swore allegiance to his
elder son William, or in the event of his death, which
occurred the following year, to the infant Henry.
Mortimer's strongholds were invested and, after some
resistance, reduced, he himself making his peace with
the king at Bridgnorth early in July.

With the collapse of Mortimer's rebellion all active
opposition to the king ceased. Henry, Bishop of
Winchester, brother of the late King Stephen, having
possibly displayed his sympathy with the defeated
party too prominently, deemed it prudent to retire
to the Continent, leaving his castles to share the fate
of other private fortresses. Peace being thus ensured
in England, King Henry was at liberty to look abroad,
and at a council held in Winchester at Michaelmas he
broached the subject of the conquest of Ireland, proposing to subdue that turbulent and uncivilised
country and place it under the rule of his brother
William. To strengthen his position and justify his
action he sent John of Salisbury to represent to
the pope the urgent need for reform, ecclesiastical
and political, in Ireland. The pope at this time,
Adrian IV., was an Englishman, his father being a
poor clerk of Langley, who entered the monastery of
St. Albans shortly after his son's birth : the young
Nicholas Brakespere, endeavouring to follow his
father's example, was rejected by the authorities at
St. Albans and went out of England to Provence,

where he rose to be abbot of St. Ruphus; his monks, regretting their election of a foreigner, appealed to the pope to depose him, and he again prospered by rejection, as he was at once promoted to the bishopric of Albano and made papal legate to Scandinavia, where his success was so great that, upon the death of Pope Eugenius III., in December 1154, he was elected to the papacy, taking the title of Adrian IV. Pope Adrian heartily approved of Henry's project, and sent back John of Salisbury with a letter commending the proposed crusade and an emerald ring symbolic of the sovereignty of Ireland, with which he invested Henry by virtue of the alleged supremacy of the popes over all islands.[1] Feeling in England, however, does not seem to have been in favour of the expedition, and the empress, doubtless foreseeing that William would find the Irish throne an insecure position of little glory and less profit, strongly opposed the project. Her influence with her son was sufficient to cause him to abandon the idea, or at least to postpone it until a more favourable opportunity.

Henry kept Christmas at Westminster, and early in January 1156 sailed from Dover for Normandy, his last act before leaving being to re-create Aubrey de Vere, who the previous year had paid 500 marks to be High Chamberlain of England,[2] Earl of Oxford.

[1] The claim of the popes to the sovereignty over islands was based upon the forged " Donation " of Constantine.

[2] This payment of 500 marks, entered under Essex on the lost Pipe Roll for the first year of Henry II., is copied into the *Red Book of the Exchequer.*

At the beginning of the next month he met Louis VII.
on the borders of France and Normandy and did
homage to him for all his continental possessions,
including Anjou and Maine, which his brother Geoffrey
claimed under his father's will. Geoffrey, persisting
in his claims and refusing Henry's offers of compensation, garrisoned his castles of Loudun, Chinon,
and Mirabeau. By the beginning of July the two
latter were in the king's hands, and Geoffrey had
agreed to be content with retaining Loudun and a
money pension. Shortly afterwards the people of
Nantes and Lower Brittany expelled their ruler,
Count Hoel, and elected Geoffrey in his place. Henry
gladly assented to the election, and upon Geoffrey's
death in 1158 successfully enforced his own claims,
as heir to his brother, against Conan, Earl of Richmond and Count of Upper Brittany.

The king's first daughter, Maud, had been born at
London early in the summer, and towards the end
of August Queen Eleanor crossed from England and
joined her husband in Anjou The court returned
to England in April 1157, and a short tour was
made through the eastern counties, the king wearing his crown in state at Bury St. Edmunds on
19th May and staying the following week at Colchester. In continuation of his former policy he
now caused William de Warenne, Earl of Surrey,
to surrender the castles of Norwich and Pevensey,
which he had hitherto retained, apparently compen-
sating him by further additions to his great estates

in Norfolk.[1] Earl Hugh of Norfolk was also deprived of his castles, and in Essex one of Earl Geoffrey's strongholds was destroyed.

Henry was now so firmly established on the throne that he could insist upon a far more important resumption of territory, and accordingly he demanded from the young King Malcolm of Scotland the cession of Northumberland, Westmoreland, and Cumberland. Malcolm, unable to offer any effective resistance to his demands, travelled south through Yorkshire and Lincolnshire to the castle of the Peak. Meanwhile Henry, after holding a council on 17th July at Northampton, where he left the queen, was moving westwards. The two kings met at the Peak and passed on together to Chester, where Malcolm formally restored the northern counties, receiving in exchange the earldom of Huntingdon, for which he did homage to Henry. The Scottish king then returned to his own country to repress the rebellion raised by his nobles in indignation at his surrender to the English demands, while Henry completed his arrangements for the invasion of North Wales.

[1] There are numerous references to the " nova terra " of Earl Warenne on the Pipe Roll 4 Henry II.

CHAPTER III

THE WELSH WARS

THE Welsh, who had been brought into at least nominal subjection by the strong hand of Henry I., were not slow to avail themselves of England's weakness under Stephen to regain their liberty. Unfortunately the chief result of the removal of foreign control was the increase of those internal disputes which had always formed so large a part of the nation's history.[1] Prince warred with prince, brother against brother, and cousin against cousin; treachery was met with treachery, and in the end the inevitable appeal of a disappointed claimant for foreign assistance against his successful rival brought an English army into Welsh soil once more. Owain Gwynedd, king of North Wales, had exiled his brother Cadwalader and seized his possessions, and it was on the pretext of restoring Cadwalader that Henry assembled his forces at Chester and prepared for the invasion of Wales in the summer of 1157.

The task was formidable alike from the nature of the country and the inhabitants. Wales .was

[1] According to the *Brut y Tywysogion* (p. 109), an English governor on one occasion took certain action, " knowing the manners of the people of the country, that they would all be killing one another."

26

divided into three parts—North Wales or Vene-
dotia, South Wales or Demetia, and Powys, but,
save that the lance was the weapon of the northern
Welsh and the bow of the southern, the divisions were
arbitrary and artificial, and unconnected with any
differences in the character of the population. With
the exception of the Brabantine mercenaries, a race
apart, a tribe of professional Ishmaelites, ready to
turn their hands against any man for pay, no nation
was so thoroughly permeated by the martial spirit
as the Welsh. With the English and Normans war
was the business of the gentry, but throughout
Wales the young men of all classes, gentle and
peasant alike, devoted their leisure to the practice
of military exercises and strove to perfect themselves
in the art of war. Possessing a country whose woods
and mountains, intersected by torrents and marshy
valleys, were admirably adapted for the ambuscade
and other tricks of guerilla warfare, the Welsh had
cultivated those qualities which enabled them to
make best use of these natural advantages. Simple
in their requirements for food or dress, they were
hardy, active, and endowed with wonderful powers of
endurance. Of defensive armour they made practically no use, yet they did not hesitate to encounter
any foe, however well equipped ; their first attack,
delivered to an accompaniment of yells and braying
trumpets, was furious, but, as is inevitable when
light armed troops engage with heavy, if it did not
prove immediately successful, they soon broke and

fled, always ready, however, to resume the fight
if opportunity offered. They did not disdain to
strengthen their position with fortifications, and the
whole land bristled with castles,[1] hardly a year passing without record of the erection, capture, recapture,
or destruction of one or more castles in the course
of the incessant wars waged either between local
chieftains or with the Norman barons of the Marches ;
yet it was emphatically in the strategical use which
they made of the natural advantages of their country
that the Welsh were pre-eminent.

It is possible that the straightforward pitched
battle between troops contending stubbornly under
the open sky tends to promote the honourable tradi-
tions of chivalry, while the ambush, surprise, and
night attack foster treachery and deceit. Certain
it is that the Welsh were notorious amongst their
contemporaries as liars and perjurers, men to whom
the most solemn oaths were not binding; and their
Norman neighbours, the lords Marchers, were not
slow to follow their example, so that the history of
the border warfare is constantly stained with treachery and broken oaths. The corollary to " Taffy
was a Welshman " that " Taffy was a thief " was
already recognised as an axiom at the time of the
Domesday Survey, when the customs of the Herefordshire Welsh contained provisions for correcting
this reprehensible propensity. Yet in spite of this

---

[1] Many of these were probably merely positions of advantage
strengthened with ditch and wooden stockade.

tendency to enrich themselves at the expense of
their neighbours the Welsh were open handed and
generous ; none need beg for a meal, nor need the
wayfarer fear to lack a resting-place. Hospitality
was not so much a duty as a commonplace of life
amongst this people, and exercised without hesitation. The food was simple, for though orgies of
gluttony and drunkenness were only too common
after a successful plundering raid, yet the habitual
excess prevalent in England was here unknown ; but
this simplicity was more than atoned for by the charms
of female society and the delights of music. In
music the Welsh surpassed even the Irish ; in every
house a harp was to be found, and it is noteworthy
that they shared with the men of Yorkshire the
peculiarity of singing not in unison but in parts. In
their rhythmical chanted songs the nation's exceptional powers of rhetoric found their highest form
of expression, and their bards were held in such
honour that in 1157, when Morgan, son of King
Owain Gwynedd, was murdered, it is expressly noted
that with him was slain Gwrgant ap Rhys, " the best
poet." Thus with music and eloquent conversation
were passed the restful hours of the day, the remainder of which would be devoted to military
exercise, hunting, the tending of flocks and herds,
or, more rarely, agriculture, for which the poor soil
and the inclinations of the people were alike un-
suited. They were thus perilously dependent upon
England for much of their food supply and therefore

liable to be starved · into surrender in the event
of war.

The antagonism existing between the peoples of
England and Wales found some echo in the relations
between the two branches of the Church. The
Welsh Church, possessing a far longer continuous
history than that of England, was less completely
under the influence of Rome, and retained many
primitive customs which were strange and even
abhorrent to the more orthodox   Their clergy continued to marry, with the result that many benefices
had become hereditary, descending from father to
son like secular property.   But if the marriage of the
clergy was a primitive condition no longer canonical,
the marriage customs of the laity were still more
shocking to the orthodox, being in many cases not
merely uncanonical but clearly survivals from pagan
times, indefensible on any grounds except those of
crude common-sense.   The English Church, having
control of the four sees of St. David's, Llandaff,
Bangor, and St. Asaph, should have been able to
execute the necessary reforms, but unfortunately
Norman prejudice forbade the appointment of a
Welshman to any post of authority in Wales, and
the sees were consequently occupied by foreigners
who, for the most part, could not speak the language
of their flocks, and only too frequently used their power
to increase their slender revenues at the expense of
their clergy. Despised by the Norman clergy as
corrupt and by the nobles as barbarous, it is possible

that the Welsh appeared to Henry less formidable opponents than they really were. Moreover, he disregarded the advice of the lords of the Marches, whose whole lives were spent in fighting their Welsh neighbours, and determined to conduct his expedition on the most approved continental lines. Owain had entrenched himself at Basingwerk, and Henry accordingly advanced along the coast for some distance, and then, meditating a flanking movement, led a detachment of his forces through the woods of Consillt. This gave the Welsh the opportunity for which they had been waiting, and no sooner were the Normans entangled in the woods than the forces under Owain's sons, David and Cynan, fell upon them, inflicting heavy losses. Caught at a disadvantage the invaders were thrown into confusion; two of their leaders, Eustace Fitz-John and Robert de Courcy, were slain, and a cry was raised that the king had been killed. Panic ensued, and it was afterwards said that Henry of Essex, the Constable of England, had thrown down the royal standard and fled. If the Constable really displayed cowardice on this occasion the fact must have been hushed up, for nothing is heard of it for six years, until in 1163 Robert de Montfort made it the subject of a formal accusation. Such an accusation could have only one outcome, and accordingly a duel was fought between the two parties at Reading in the king's presence, when Henry of Essex, rashly abandoning a successful defence for the offensive, was defeated and left for

dead on the ground, but being nursed back to life
by the monks of Reading, joined their community
and spent the remainder of his days in their abbey.
It is noteworthy that the challenger, Robert de
Montfort, was a connection of his opponent's and
not improbably a rival claimant to the constableship, which Henry had inherited through the heiress
of Hugh de Montfort.[1] On the whole it would seem
more probable that Robert should have made his
accusation as a taunt based on some flying rumour
and that the result of the duel was unjust, than that
King Henry should have condoned the Constable's
cowardice and allowed him to continue in honour
at his court.

However Henry of Essex may have behaved, it is
clear that the Normans had suffered a severe defeat,
and Henry in a furious rage drew off his troops and
rejoined the main body of his army, with which he
advanced unopposed to Rhuddlan, Owain having
withdrawn from Basingwerk to Conway. Meanwhile
the fleet, which was acting in unison with the land
forces, had been despatched to Anglesea, to ravage
that fertile island, the granary of North Wales. But
here bad discipline was the cause of a severe check ;
the attractions of looting churches and monasteries
proved too great for the royal forces and delivered
them into the hands of the ever vigilant natives.
The sailors lost their commander, William Tren-
chemer, and most of their officers, while amongst

[1] See Round, *Commune of London*, 281.

the men of note who fell was Henry, the king's half-
uncle, son of Henry I. by the famous Welsh princess
Nest.   In spite of these two initial successes Owain
felt himself in a position of danger, and preferring
to make terms rather than to have them forced upon
him, made peace and gave hostages to Henry.   Cadwalader was restored to his possessions, and homage
was done by Owain to the English king, and the
English frontier was once more pushed as far forward
as Rhuddlan, where, as also at Basingwerk, Henry
restored the castle.   The campaign, therefore, might
be regarded as fairly successful, although the only
two engagements recorded had been disastrous.

Although Owain Gwynedd and the other princes
had come to terms with King Henry, the redoubtable
Rhys, son of Gruffudd of South Wales, proposed to
continue the war.   Finding, however, that he would
receive no support from any other native princes,
he was persuaded to make his peace with the king,
who in return promised to grant him a complete
cantref of land.   The spirit of the agreement was
broken by the grant of the land in scattered portions
instead of in a continuous block, but Rhys accepted
the gift and remained quiet until he found that the
king would not do him justice against Walter Clifford,
when he took the law into his own hands and made
a series of successful attacks upon the strongholds of
the Norman barons in Cardigan.   About the same
time, in 1158, Yvor the Little, a noble of Glamorgan,
being deprived of his lands by Earl William of

Gloucester, made a daring night attack upon the castle of Cardiff, and in spite of its strength and the imposing numbers of its garrison, said to have numbered 120 men-at-arms, besides archers and others, carried off the earl with his countess and their son, who were only released after more than full restitution had been made to Yvor. Meanwhile Rhys, encouraged by his successes in Cardigan, attacked Caermarthen, and Henry, who was preparing for a great expedition into the south of France, was obliged to send a force under the Earls of Cornwall, Gloucester, and Clare to relieve the castle. This they did, and they were also successful in bringing Rhys to accept terms of peace.

Peace, so far as it ever existed on the Welsh borders, continued for a short time, but when Henry returned to England in 1163, he found the country in so disturbed a state that he was obliged to lead an army against Rhys. The latter offered little or no active opposition, and the expedition took the form of a military progress through Glamorgan and Gower towards Caermarthen and as far as Pencader, returning by the mountains of Plinlimmon to Radnor. It is said that during this progress the invading host came to a stream called Nant Pencarn, where the natives anxiously waited to see whether Henry would fulfil in his own person a traditional prophecy that the crossing of the ancient ford by a brave man with a freckled face should foreshadow the defeat of the Welsh. When they saw the king ride past the

old ford and set his horse to cross by one newer and
better known, the Welsh set up such a blare of horns
and trumpets that his horse took fright, and the
king, turning round, made for the older ford and
dashed across, this time without any orchestral
welcome.

As a result of this campaign Rhys, with Owain of
North Wales and other princes, attended Henry's
court at Woodstock and did homage to him there
in July 1163. The king, apparently meditating the
confiscation of his estates or possibly the extortion
of a ransom, sent a knight to visit Dynevor, the capital
of South Wales, and to report upon the nature of the
country ; the priest, however, who acted as guide,
while professing to go by the best route, took the
unsuspecting knight by all the worst and most impassable tracks, and so contrived to impress him with
the utter poverty of the land and the inhabitants
that the king, on the strength of his report, abandoned his first intention and released Rhys, only
taking from him hostages for his good behaviour.
Hardly had Rhys returned than he renewed the
struggle, recapturing the whole district of Cardigan,
invading Pembrokeshire and despoiling the Norman
and Flemish settlers. His example was speedily
followed by Owain Gwynedd and his sons, who
ravaged the district round Rhuddlan. In October
1164 Henry had issued orders for a force to be raised
against Rhys, and on his return to England in the
following May, he found this force ready and with it

pushed hastily forward to Rhuddlan. Having relieved pressure in this district for the time being he
returned to England to collect a larger army, furiously
vowing to destroy the whole nation of Welsh. The
border fortresses were set in order from Abergavenny,
Grosmont, Llantilis, and Skenfrith in the south to
Montgomery, Shrawardine, and Chirk in the north ;
foreign mercenaries were brought over and provided
with arms, Ernald the armourer providing 300
bucklers for their use; lances and arrows were bought
in Oxford and elsewhere and despatched to the
frontier ; and, above all, large sums of money were
extorted from the cities, prelates, and nobles for the
conduct of the war.[1] Operations on a small scale
seem to have been carried on from Abergavenny,
but the king, with the main part of his imposing
army, advanced from Shrewsbury to Oswestry and so
into Powys. For once the Welsh were united ; Rhys
of South Wales, Owain Gwynedd and Cadwalader his
brother, the former ally of the English, the two sons
of Madog of Powys, lesser princes such as Owain
Cyveliog and Jorwerth the Red, all with their whole
following were assembled to oppose the invader.

Henry advanced down the valley of the Ceiriog
and, mindful of former disaster, endeavoured to protect his flanks by cutting down the woods. In-
decisive skirmishing took place, resulting in heavy
losses to both sides, but the Welsh avoided a pitched

---

[1] Details of these proceedings are to be found on the Pipe Rolls,
11 and 12 Henry II.

battle and retired before the royal forces until the latter had penetrated as far as the mountains of Berwyn in Merionethshire. Here they encamped, ravaging the country round and plundering the churches, to the intense anger of the Welsh, who always scrupulously observed the sanctity of churches. Punishment speedily overtook the impious host: tremendous storms of rain, exceptionally vehement even for Wales, coupled with a shortage of provisions, drove the English back in a disorderly and disastrous retreat to Chester, where Henry waited for the arrival of a fleet from Ireland. When the ships came they proved to be insufficient for the conduct of further operations against the Welsh. The king, furious at his ill-success, took a mean revenge by barbarously mutilating the sons of Rhys and Owain and a score of other hostages in his power.[1]

Hardly had the English army retired from Wales when Rhys stormed the castle of Cardigan and captured its lord, Robert Fitz-Stephen. Next year, in 1165, the Normans and Flemings of Pembroke made two unsuccessful attempts to retake Cardigan, while in the north Owain Gwynedd destroyed Basingwerk. Internal dissensions led to the ejection from their lands of Jorwerth the Red and Owain Cyveliog,[2] and

---

[1] In justice to Henry it must be remembered that the mutilation or execution of hostages was the natural outcome of the rebellion of those for whose good conduct they were sureties. A hostage who cannot be punished for the sins of those whom he represents is merely a useless expense to his keeper.

[2] The Pipe Roll, 12 Henry II., shows both these princes on good terms with the English.

the latter, in 1166, assisted the Normans to gain a small success in the capture of the castle of Caereinion, but this was more than counterbalanced by the action of Rhys and Owain Gwynedd, who, after a three months' siege, captured the castles of Rhuddlan and Prestatyn. The development of Irish affairs now made friendly relations with Wales important, the main route to Ireland being by way of South Wales and the ports of Pembrokeshire. Accordingly we find Henry becoming reconciled to Rhys in 1171, and from henceforth treating him with an honourable courtesy which the Welsh prince reciprocated. Peace, therefore, varied with occasional border skirmishes, continued between England and Wales until the end of Henry's reign, and the Welsh, deprived of the pleasure of molesting the foreigner, turned with the greater zest to the task of cutting one another's throats.

The invariable failure of Henry's military policy in Wales was due to his persistent disregard of the local lords of the marches and reliance upon men famous in continental warfare but totally ignorant of the very different conditions prevailing in the mountains and forests of Wales. Such a man as Gerald de Barri could have given the king far more useful advice in the conduct of a Welsh campaign than any of his great Norman barons. That acute historian afterwards set out at length the measures necessary for the conquest of his native country. No expedition should be undertaken hastily, but careful preparations should be made, allies secured, and internal divisions carefully fostered ; castles should be built along the frontier, trade with England, especially in provisions, stopped, and the coasts blockaded. This would, as a rule, be sufficient to bring them to terms, but if military operations were needful then an advance should be made in the early spring before the trees came into leaf ; the troops should be light armed, and preferably men of the border used to the country rather than Flemish or Brabantines, good as the latter were on their own ground. The operations should be conducted by counsel of the lords marchers, and heavy losses must be expected and borne with equanimity, for while mercenaries are easily replaced the Welsh could not replace their men. Once subdued the natives should be treated with justice and kindness so long as they remain quiet, but their rulers should be ever watchful and should punish rebellion with severity. To diminish the chance of revolt the intervals of peace ought to be used for the building of roads and of castles, and at the same time the English border towns along the Severn might well have special privileges granted them to facilitate their growth, and in return they should be bound to maintain a fitting provision of arms and horses and to practise universal military training. " Yet for all this the nation shall not perish utterly, and at the last great Day of Judgment this little spot of land shall be answered for by the Welsh race, still speaking in their ancient tongue."

CHAPTER IV

FOREIGN AFFAIRS

AFTER the ingloriously successful Welsh campaign of 1157 Henry seems to have returned to Woodstock and there rejoined the queen, who had given birth on 8th September to a third son, Richard. The remainder of the autumn was no doubt spent in hunting, but at the end of the year the court moved northwards to Lincoln, where Christmas was kept. A local tradition, or superstition, forbade the wearing of the royal crown within the city walls. Stephen, it is true, had defied this tradition in 1146, but the fortunes of Stephen were not such as to make his action an encouraging precedent, and Henry, preferring to be on the safe side, caused the ceremonial of coronation to take place in the church of St. Mary of Wigford outside the walls. From Lincoln the king moved on, at the beginning of 1158, to Carlisle to meet Malcolm of Scotland. The result of the meeting was unsatisfactory, and Henry abandoned his original intention of bestowing upon the young king that honour of knighthood which he had himself once received at the hands of Malcolm's predecessor, David.

Easter in that year fell on 20th April, when the

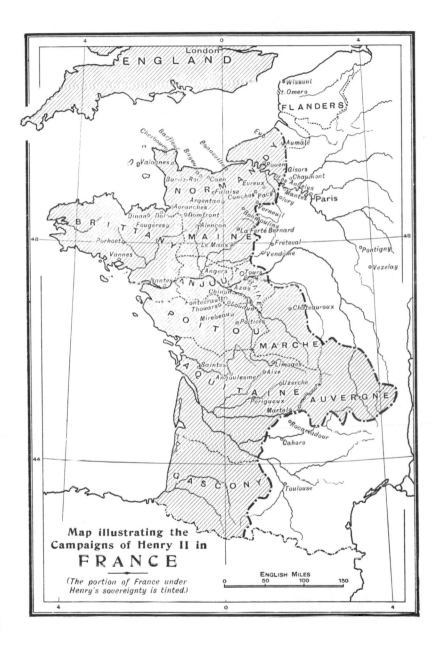

Map illustrating the
Campaigns of Henry II in
FRANCE

(The portion of France under
Henry's sovereignty is tinted.)

ENGLISH MILES
0   50   100   150

court was at Worcester, and Henry and Eleanor celebrated the festival by observing, for the last time, the elaborate ritual of coronation. When the service was over they laid their crowns upon the altar and vowed to wear them no more. There would seem to have been no deeper reason for this renunciation than Henry's dislike of ceremony. To the restless king, who never sat except on the saddle and who whispered and scribbled notes to relieve the boredom of Mass, the elaborate ceremonial of the crown-wearing must have been distasteful and wearisome. The outward pomp and circumstance of royalty were nothing to the man whose rule extended from the Pennines to the Pyrenees, and the glitter of a crown was no enhancement to the clearest head in Europe, throbbing full with political problems, national and international. The kings of Wales and Scotland had done homage; Godred, King of Man and the Isles, was in attendance at Worcester; embassies had been received or were on their way from the kings of Norway, the King of Jerusalem, and the Emperor Frederic; and Henry was scheming for the further aggrandisement of his family and the extension of his continental dominions.

Louis VII. had by his second wife, Constance of Castille, a daughter Margaret, at this time a baby of a few months old, and Henry determined to forestall other possible aspirants for the hand of this very youthful heiress. Accordingly, in the summer of 1158, he despatched his chancellor, Thomas Becket,

to demand the hand of Margaret for his eldest surviving son, Henry, who was now rather more than
two years old.   If the king was inclined to underrate
the value of display and outward magnificence, his
chancellor was very far from falling into the same
error.   Becket, the king's trusted minister and most
intimate friend, presented a curious contrast in every
way to his royal master.   He was tall, of command-
ing presence, with clean-cut features and shapely
hands ;   in his splendour he was a prototype of
Cardinal Wolsey, but stood out the more prominently,
as the sober court of Henry II. made a better foil
than the magnificence of Henry VIII.   Intensely
self-centred, whatever he took up he threw himself
into heart and soul, and as he was to prove the
most ecclesiastical of ecclesiastics, so now that he
was the greatest officer in the land he saw to it that
his dignity was becomingly supported.   Lavish in his
expenditure, he kept open house and enriched his
friends with open-handed generosity.   Yet, though
luxury and ostentation formed the note of his household, it is to his honour that in an age when views
on morals were more than lax he was known pre-
eminently as a man of clean life.

The embassy to the French court presented Becket
with an admirable opportunity for gratifying his
taste for pageantry, and the splendour of his cavalcade struck amazement into the minds of the natives
and impressed them with the greatness of the English
king.   In front of the procession came the serving

men and lackeys on foot in groups of ten or a dozen
singing English songs, and some way behind them
came huntsmen leading dogs and with their grey-
hounds in leash ; then there rattled over the stones
six great covered waggons containing the baggage
of the chancellor's household, and two other waggons
loaded solely with the very best English ale as a
present for the French. Each of these carts was
drawn by five magnificent horses, each attended by
its own groom, and as guard to each cart was a great
mastiff. Next came the pack horses with their
drivers, and as a picturesque touch there sat upon
the back of each horse an ape or monkey. After
these came the squires, some carrying the shields of
their masters and leading their chargers, others
bearing hawks and falcons ; then the officers of the
household, and the knights and clerks riding two and
two, and finally the chancellor himself with his
friends. Becket did not allow the effect of his
arrival to be diminished by any failure to maintain
his state during his stay in Paris, and the extravagance and luxury of his household at the Temple,
which had been assigned for his accommodation,
became proverbial. And when the business of his
mission had been successfully settled he distributed
all his gold and silver plate, his furs and gorgeous
robes, horses and the other magnificent appointments of his establishment in lavish largesse.

Henry followed close on the heels of his splendid
ambassador to complete the negotiations for the

proposed matrimonial alliance. The two kings met
first on the borders of France and Normandy, near
Gisors, and Henry then paid a formal visit to Louis
in Paris, where his unassuming courtesy and refusal
of all ceremonial honours made an impression quite
as favourable as the magnificence of his chancellor
had done. Not only did Louis fall in with the
suggestion for the betrothal of Margaret to the young
Henry, but he also agreed to assist the English king
in his claim on the territory of Nantes and Lower
Brittany. Geoffrey, Henry's younger brother, had
held this province for life by the election of the
inhabitants, but upon his death in July 1158, Conan,
Count of Brittany, claimed that it should revert to
him. In face of the united forces of England and
France Conan could only submit, surrendering Nantes
in return for a confirmation of his rights in the
remainder of Brittany. After taking over Nantes
Henry led a brilliant little expedition against Thouars,
in Poitou, capturing that strong position and its
rebellious lord with surprising rapidity, and then,
turning north, met King Louis at Le Mans, accompanied him on a pilgrimage to St. Michael's Mount,
and entertained him for some time at Rouen. Thanks
to the French king's good offices several favourable
arrangements were made for the surrender of border
castles to Henry, and it was with satisfaction that
Henry could look back upon the recent results of his
diplomacy when he celebrated the feast of Christmas
that year at Cherbourg with Queen Eleanor, who

SEAL OF LOUIS VII (½)

had given birth to her fourth son, Geoffrey, in the
previous September.

His policy having so far met with such remarkable
success Henry now decided to revive his wife's ancient
and shadowy claim to the important province of
Toulouse.   This province had been sold by one of
Queen Eleanor's ancestors to his brother, Raymond
of St. Gilles, but the legality of the sale had been
questioned on more than one occasion, and Louis VII.,
at the time that Eleanor was his wife, had prepared
to enforce his claim, but had come to an amicable
agreement with the Count of St. Gilles, giving him
to wife his sister Constance, widow of King Stephen's
son Eustace.   Henry now made warlike preparations
on an unprecedented scale, securing as an ally Raymond Berenger, virtual King of Arragon and Duke
of Provence but proudly content to be known by his
humbler ancestral title of Count of Barcelona, and
calling on all his fiefs, English and continental, for
aids of men and money. In the imposing army
which marched upon Toulouse in July 1159, practically all the great barons of England and Normandy
were present with their retinues, the chancellor as
usual outshining his peers in the number and splendour
of his knights. Malcolm of Scotland came with a
band of his young nobles, and was rewarded by
Henry with the coveted honour of knighthood, and
there was one of the Welsh princes; but the main
body of the troops consisted of Welsh and other
mercenaries, hired with the money wrung from the

great prelates, the larger towns, and the Jews and
other wealthy non-combatants. Such a force could
easily have captured Toulouse, but King Louis had
hastened to the aid of his brother-in-law and was
within the town. For Henry to attack would therefore mean a direct assault upon the man who, as King
of France, was technically his over-lord and suzerain,
a breach of feudal law which Henry, to the disgust
of Becket and other less scrupulous men, refused to
commit. The only alternative was a blockade, and
this proving futile and ineffectual the great army
withdrew at the end of September, having achieved
practically nothing but the capture of Cahors. On
his way north, however, Henry was able to induce
the Count of Evreux to hand over the castles of
Montfort, Epernon, and Rochfort, and Louis, finding
his lines of communication thus cut, hastily concluded
peace.

During this war Pope Adrian had died, and Cardinal
Roland Bandinelli had been elected by a majority of
the electoral college, and, after a little hesitation, had
accepted the papacy under the title of Alexander III. ;
the party of the Emperor Frederic, however, taking
advantage of Roland's hesitation, had declared their
candidate, Octavian, elected, and had consecrated
him pope as Victor III. The question of which pope
should be recognised was discussed at councils held
by Henry at Neufmarché in Normandy and by Louis
at Beauvais, and in each case the decision was given
in favour of Alexander, Victor being renounced as

schismatic.   This result was largely due to the eloquence of Alexander's legate, Cardinal William of
Pavia.   He, with Cardinal Henry of Pisa, was at the
English king's court at the end of October 1160,
when the news arrived that Louis, within a fortnight
of his wife's death, had, in his eagerness to obtain
an heir to his throne, married a sister of Theobald,
Count of Blois.   Henry at once persuaded the cardinals to celebrate the marriage between his son
Henry, not yet five years old, and the French king's
daughter Margaret, then in her third year ;   the
marriage having thus been performed with the consent of the Church, as stipulated in his treaty with
Louis, Henry was entitled to demand as Margaret's
marriage portion the surrender of the Norman Vexin
and its castles of Gisors, Néaufles, and Neufchâtel,
which he accordingly received from the three Templars who were acting as trustees of the settlement.

This piece of sharp practice roused the resentment
of Louis, but Henry's defences were too strong for any
effective military operations, and, after some desultory
skirmishing on the borders, peace was patched up in
the summer of 1162 and continued without actual
breach for some five years.   At the end of that time,
in June 1167, Henry's interference in the affairs of
Auvergne afforded Louis excuse for a fresh campaign,
whose prospects of success were the greater from its
coincidence, no doubt designed, with a rising on an
unusually large scale amongst the unruly Breton

nobles. The French accordingly ravaged the Norman border, but Henry virtually brought the campaign to an end by a single brilliant stroke. Knowing the provisions and munitions of the French army had been stored at Chaumont, he marched against that town, and while his men-at-arms engaged the garrison outside the walls his light-armed Welsh levies swam down the river and, gaining access to the town by that unexpected quarter, set it on fire. The whole town was destroyed, many of its defenders slain or captured, and the rest driven into the castle, where Henry left them unmolested, content with the destruction of the stores. Although this practically put an end to hostilities, no peace could be arranged until the French king's impotent rage had been appeased, and the brilliant suggestion was therefore made by the Empress Maud that he should be allowed to burn some unfortified Norman town. Les Andelys was selected as the victim; the inhabitants were duly warned by Henry to leave the place, and the French army solemnly marched on the deserted town and burnt it. Having cheaply regained his honour by this puerile act of revenge, Louis agreed, in August 1168, to a six months' truce. This gave Henry time to suppress the rising in Brittany and another in Poitou, while the refractory counts of Ponthieu and Perche received their chastisement during the ensuing negotiations, varied with occasional fighting, which resulted at last in a definite treaty of peace being concluded between the two

kings in January 1169. By this treaty it was agreed
that Henry's son, Richard, should be betrothed to the
French king's daughter, Alais, and should hold Poitou
and Guienne, while Geoffrey, who had married Count
Conan's daughter in 1166, should hold Brittany
under his elder brother Henry.

Henry's two eldest sons were thus married or
betrothed to daughters of King Louis and his third
son married to the heiress of Brittany ; the youngest,
John, having only been born on Christmas Eve, 1166,
was not yet provided for, but the king's eldest
daughter, Maud, had sailed from Dover in the
autumn of 1167, under the escort of the Arch-
bishop-elect of Cologne, the Earls of Arundel and
Pembroke, and such lesser lords as Reynold de
Warenne and William Cheyney, to marry Henry,
Duke of Saxony. Thus by the power of the sword
and the bond of marriage did Henry strengthen his
position on the Continent.

CHAPTER V

THE STRUGGLE WITH BECKET

DURING the time that Henry was campaigning on the Norman borders, in April 1161, Archbishop Theobald of Canterbury died. For nearly a year the king kept the primacy vacant, but at last, in the spring of 1162, he declared his wish that Becket should take the archiepiscopate. The appointment, not unforeseen, of the courtly chancellor seems to have been distasteful to many of the clergy, but the only man who had the courage to brave the king's wrath by opposing the election of his favourite was Gilbert Foliot, Bishop of Hereford, whose opposition was probably increased in vehemence but diminished in effect by the fact that he was himself Becket's most dangerous rival in the race for the primacy. Foliot's protest was supported by the Empress Maud, who, as a devoted daughter of the Church, doubtless considered Becket too lax and worldly for the post; but for once Henry disregarded his mother's opinion. Becket himself must have seen in his promotion the chance of satisfying his ambition; as chancellor he was the second man in the realm, subject only to the king; but, subject to him, often directing the royal policy, but always liable to be checked by an expression of the royal will ; as archbishop, with the divine authority of the Church behind him, it would be for him to dictate and for the king to obey.   Yet knowing, as he alone knew, the ultra-clerical course which he intended to take, he foresaw that it must sooner or later bring him into collision with Henry, and forebodings for the future, more particularly regret for the inevitable disruption of the ancient bonds of friendship which bound him to the king, made him hesitate to grasp the prize for which he longed.   At last the insistence of the king, coupled with the persuasions of Cardinal Henry of Pisa, overcame Becket's half-hearted resistance, and in May 1162 he sailed for England for consecration.

Besides the business attendant on his elevation to the primacy, the chancellor was charged with the carrying out of arrangements for an expedition against the Welsh and also with the performance of fealty to the king's eldest son, Henry.   The prince, who was at this time eight years old, had been entrusted by his father to Becket's care, and a very genuine feeling of affection existed between the boy and his guardian, which was to continue, unaffected by the events of later years, until the archbishop's death.   It was therefore not unsuitable that the last recorded act of Becket in his official capacity as chancellor was to head the assembled peers at Westminster in taking the oath of fealty to the young Henry. On the occasion of this ceremony, which seems to have included an informal coronation—for a golden

crown and regalia were made for the prince [1]—Becket
was formally elected to the see of Canterbury. The
right of the monks of Christ Church, Canterbury, to
appoint the archbishop, who was also nominally
their abbot, was so far recognised that they were
directed by the king's messengers, the Bishops of
Chichester, Exeter, and Rochester, Richard de Lucy
and his brother the Abbot of Battle, to hold an
election, but they were told definitely that their choice
must fall on the chancellor. This formality over,
there arose the question of consecration. The right
to perform this ceremony was disputed between
Roger, Archbishop of York, as primate, the Bishop
of Rochester as Vicar of Canterbury, and the Bishop
of Winchester as Precentor of Canterbury, while a
claim was also put in by the bishop of one of the
Welsh sees as the senior member of the episcopal
bench. The see of London, whose bishop, as Dean
of Canterbury, would have had the best claim to
officiate, was vacant, but the dean and canons
appointed Henry, Bishop of Winchester, to act for
them, and to him eventually was assigned the honour
of officiating.

On Saturday, 2nd June, Becket, who was still in
deacons' orders, was ordained priest, and on the

---

[1] The Pipe Roll for 8 Henry II. shows " 60s. paid to William Cade
for gold for the crown of the king's son, and for preparing the regalia,"
and the Roll for the twelfth year records the expenditure of 7s. " for
carrying the regalia of the king's son into Normandy." It would
also seem (see below, p. 91) that the pope issued a commission for
the Archbishop of York to crown the young prince.

following day he was consecrated archbishop. To commemorate the occasion he ordained that the Sunday following Whitsunday should in future be kept as a great festival in honour of the Holy Trinity,[1] and even the zeal of the Reformers against the cult of Thomas of Canterbury did not blot out from the calendar of the English Church Trinity Sunday.

The consecration of Thomas as Archbishop of Canterbury was indeed an event worthy of commemoration, forming as it did the prelude to the struggle between clerical and lay power which was to occupy the next ten years of Henry's reign. This struggle presents a curious problem of historical perspective. Seen through the atmosphere of the contemporary chronicle or through the rarified medium of history the Becket controversy presents very different features. To contemporaries it seemed of overpowering importance, eclipsing all other events of the time and entailing issues of enormous weight. To us the points at issue seem of slight significance, while the results appear almost negligible in comparison with the energy and heat expended to produce them. Whichever view, if either, is correct, there can be no doubt of the great part played by this episode, for though in the end the contending parties were left very much where they started the casual

---

[1] Gervase of Canterbury (*Opera*, i. 171) says that Thomas instituted the feast of the Holy Trinity. It would seem that the Sunday following Whitsunday was already sacred to the Trinity, but that he gave to the feast a position which it had not held before in England, and which it did not attain on the Continent till a much later date.

results of the struggle influenced the history of the country most powerfully, so that in this controversy the incidents are of greater importance than the main matter of contention.

It is easy to be wise after the event, and Henry is constantly blamed by modern writers for having promoted Becket to the primacy and not having foreseen the consequences. Yet little reflection is required to show that nothing short of the gift of prophecy would have enabled Henry to foresee the position which Thomas was to take up. The chancellor had habitually neglected his duties as Archdeacon of Canterbury, calling down upon himself the rebukes of Archbishop Theobald, and had on several occasions shown very slight regard for the privileges of the Church. At the time of his appointment Gilbert Foliot scoffingly remarked that the king had performed a miracle, for he had converted a knightly courtier into a holy archbishop. Events proved Foliot's jest a truth, and though it was Becket who wrought the marvellous metamorphosis himself, it remained a miracle unforeshadowed in the past life or character of the man.

Thomas, who was born on 21st December 1118, was the son of Gilbert Becket by Maud his wife. His parents, who were both of Norman extraction [1] but

---

[1] The legend that the mother of Thomas was the daughter of a Saracen emir into whose hands Gilbert Becket had fallen during a pilgrimage to the Holy Land, and that, after helping Gilbert to escape, she followed him to London, is of late date and absolutely without foundation.

had settled in London before his birth, belonged to
the middle class and were comfortably off, and by
them he was sent to the school of the canons of
Merton Priory. While he was still quite young his
mother died, and not long afterwards his father, who
was in very reduced circumstances owing to losses
by fire, followed her. Fortunately for himself
Thomas, who was a good-looking boy of much promise, had attracted the attention of a powerful baron,
Richer of L'Aigle, who had been in the habit of
putting up at the Beckets' house whenever he came
up to London. Richer interested himself in the
orphan, sending him to school in London and allowing him to spend his holidays with him in the country,
presumably at his Sussex castle of Pevensey. Here
Thomas practised hunting, hawking, and other manly
sports, on one occasion nearly losing his life in the
endeavour to rescue his falcon from a mill-stream.
His patron appears to have sent him to study in
Paris, and on his return he entered the service of his
kinsman, Osbern Huitdeniers, one of the leading
citizens of London. After some three years of official
life in the city he determined to try a field more
promising for his ambitions. Once again his father's
hospitality proved the means of his advancement,
two of Gilbert's former guests, the Archdeacon Baldwin and his brother, Master Eustace, introducing him
to the notice of Archbishop Theobald. The archbishop, finding that the young man's father had
come from his own native town of Thierceville, gladly

enrolled him in his household and took a kindly
interest in him. There were at this time at the
archbishop's court many men of distinction and
learning, and one of these, Roger of Pont l'Evêque,
afterwards Archbishop of York, jealous of the favour
shown to Thomas, whose powers lay in the direction
of showy brilliance rather than sound scholarship,
did all that he could to injure and annoy him.
Twice Roger persuaded the archbishop to dismiss
the young man, but on each occasion Theobald's
brother, Walter, Archdeacon of Canterbury, took up
his cause and secured his restoration to favour. As
early as 1143, when he was in his twenty-fifth year,
Thomas rendered his patron good service at the papal
court in the matter of annulling the legatine commission formerly granted to Bishop Henry of Winchester. About this date he appears to have attended
the famous law schools at Bologna, and afterwards at
Auxerre. By this time he was beginning to become
a person of importance; the churches of St. Mary-le-
Strand and Otford, and prebends in St. Paul's and
Lincoln had been bestowed upon him, and in March
1148 he, with his rival, Roger of Pont-l'Evêque,
attended the archbishop on his venturesome sail across
the Channel to the Council of Rheims. Three years
later, in 1151, Becket achieved a further diplomatic
success in defeating Stephen's efforts to obtain papal
recognition for his son Eustace, and in 1154, when
Roger of Pont-l'Evêque became Archbishop of York,
Thomas succeeded him as Archdeacon of Canterbury.

SEAL OF ROGER, ARCHBISHOP OF YORK (⅓)

On the accession of Henry II., as we have seen, Thomas was made chancellor by the advice of Archbishop Theobald, with the generous support of Bishop Henry of Winchester, whose claims he had once been instrumental in defeating. Of the splendour and luxury displayed in his household as chancellor something has already been said. The means to satisfy his taste for magnificence and display were furnished not only by the emoluments, regular and irregular,[1] of his office, but by multitudinous extra preferments bestowed upon him, such as the provostship of Beverley, the custody of the Tower of London, which he restored and strengthened, and the honours of Eye and Berkhamstead. He still retained his youthful love of sport and also displayed considerable military ability ; during the expedition to Toulouse he was left in command at Cahors, and justified his appointment by leading his troops in person to the capture of three other castles, while somewhat later he overthrew a French knight in single combat. The king could appreciate a man of spirit and a good sportsman, and the two men became fast friends. Henry, on his way to or from the hunt, would often drop in at the chancellor's house and take a glass of wine with him, or, vaulting the table, sit down and eat, noting with amusement the luxury for which his friend was so famous. The story is well known

---

[1] The actual salary of the chancellor was 5s. a day, but the perquisites of the office, including the gifts which those who required his favour had to make, were great. Becket himself was said, by Foliot, to have paid " many thousand marks " for the office.

how, as king and chancellor were riding together
through the streets of London one bitter winter's
day, they saw a poor old man clad in rags. Turning
to his friend the king said, "Would it not be a
meritorious act to give that poor old man a warm
cloak?" The chancellor agreeing that it would
indeed, Henry exclaimed, "You shall have the merit
of this worthy act!" and seizing Becket's magnificent fur-lined cloak, after a short struggle secured
it and flung it to the beggar.

The intimate friend of the king, a courtier, sportsman, and warrior, whose only interest in the Church
seemed to be to draw the revenues of his many benefices and to extract money from its prelates for his
royal master, no one could have foreseen Becket's
conversion into the most ultra-clerical of archbishops.

Almost the first act of the newly consecrated archbishop was to resign the chancellorship. As Becket
must have been fully aware that the king expected
him to continue in office and would never have
bestowed the primacy upon him if he had declared
his intention of resigning, his action was surprising
and unjustifiable. Henry, though deeply annoyed,
accepted the situation and displayed no ill-feeling
towards Thomas. In fact when he landed at Southampton in January 1163, having been detained at
Cherbourg over Christmas by bad weather, he greeted
the archbishop with all the warmth of affection which
he had formerly bestowed upon the chancellor. These
good relations continued for some months, Thomas

supporting the king's request to the pope for the
translation of Gilbert Foliot from Hereford to the
vacant see of London,[1] and Henry visiting the archbishop at Canterbury on his way down to Dover to
meet the Count of Flanders in March. But Becket
was now throwing himself with his usual thorough-
ness into the work appropriate to his position as
head of the English Church. His taste for display
continued unabated, but found new outlets. As
archbishop he was the recognised patron of the
younger sons of nobles as the king was of their elder
sons, while amongst the crowd of high-born youths
serving as his esquires was the heir to the throne ;
his household was as magnificent and his table as
well-appointed as ever, but the clerks, who had
formerly received little consideration, had now sup-
planted the knights in the place of honour, while a
somewhat ostentatious prominence was given to the
daily distribution of alms and feeding of large numbers
of poor persons. Thomas himself presided gracefully
over the splendid feasts, and, though far from prac-
tising the stern asceticism of Gilbert Foliot, observed
a strict moderation suitable to the monastic habit
which he had assumed; and although there was no
lack of gaiety and animation at his table the jesters
and minstrels of former days were now replaced by
readers of the Holy Scripture.

[1] Translation from one see to another, except in the case of promotion to the primacy, was extremely rare, and almost unheard of,
in England at this time.

Soon the erstwhile pluralist chancellor began to
attack the bestowal of multiple benefices upon the
king's clerks, laymen in all but name, whose sole
connection with their benefices was to draw their
revenues. So long as Becket confined himself to this
legitimate course of reform the king raised no objec-
tions, only insisting that the physician should first
heal himself by surrendering the archdeaconry of
Canterbury, which he had most inconsistently retained
with the archbishopric. But soon Thomas passed
from correcting the faults of his clergy to protecting
their vices. The complaints of the laity against the
extortions and injustice of the archdeacons and their
officials had been brought to Henry's notice in the
time of Archbishop Theobald, and one particular
case reported from Scarborough roused the king to
declare that these clerical officers wrung more money
from the people every year than the revenues of the
crown. Had not matters of importance obliged
Henry to leave England just at this time it is not
improbable that he would have carried out, with the
assistance of Thomas the Chancellor, some of those
measures for the control of the clerical courts which
Thomas the Archbishop devoted his life to opposing.
The bishops ordained candidates without regard to
their fitness, and, contrary to the canons, bestowed
orders upon men who had no title. Inevitably the
country was overrun with men of low character, without definite means of subsistence, who could laugh
alike at the lay courts, which had no jurisdiction

over them, and at the ecclesiastical courts, whose
proceedings were only too often a farce; for the
clerk who held no church deprivation had no terrors,
and it was well known that the bishops would rather
a guilty clerk were acquitted than that they should
be burdened with the cost of his keep in the episcopal
prisons.   Murders and other crimes were committed
by these bastard sons of the Church, and any attempt
to bring the offenders to book was foiled by the prelates.   Becket, who as chancellor had imprisoned a
clerk in the Tower for seduction, now threw the
mantle of the Church over an unworthy clerk who
had been guilty of a peculiarly atrocious murder and
adultery.   The king felt strongly in the matter, but
it would seem that for a time his old affection kept
him from pressing his anti-clerical measures to the
point of an actual breach with the archbishop.   Other
matters, however, more personal, now arose to increase
the estrangement between the former friends.

On his return from the Welsh expedition in July
1163, Henry appears to have found his affairs rather
involved and to have proposed to increase his revenue
by appropriating the annual payment known as the
"Sheriff's aid"; the exact points in dispute are
obscure and will be discussed in a later chapter, but
it is known that the king swore "by the eyes of God" [1]

---

[1] A small point, not without significance as an indication of character, is observable in the gradual degradation of the royal oath.
The Conqueror swore "by the splendour of God," Henry "by the
eyes of God," Richard "by the body" or "by the thighs of God,"
and John "by the feet," or even "by the nails, of God."

that the payment should be made part of the Crown
revenues and that the archbishop vowed " by his
reverence for those same eyes " that no penny of it
should be paid from his lands while he lived. In the
end Henry had to give way, and he was again defeated by Becket about the same time in another
matter still nearer to his heart. During the retreat
from Toulouse in 1159 King Stephen's son, William,
Count of Boulogne, and, in right of his wife, Earl of
Surrey and Warenne, had died, leaving no children.
To prevent the ccunty of Boulogne falling into the
hands of any adherent of the King of France, Henry
took William's sister, Mary, out of the nunnery of
Romsey, where she was abbess, and married her to
Matthew, son of the Count of Flanders, in spite of
Becket's very proper protests. Earl William's widow,
Isabel de Warenne, being still unmarried, the king
decided that her heritage would form a suitable
provision for his brother William, for whom he had
once proposed to conquer Ireland. He therefore
began to push the marriage forward, but was stopped
by the action of the archbishop, who forbade it on the
ground that the contracting parties were related
within the prohibited degrees.[1] A papal dispensation
had been available for the marriage of Abbess Mary,
but the opposition of Thomas the Archbishop proved

---

[1] Isabelle de Warenne had been the wife of William, son of King
Stephen, the cousin of William of Anjou. The connection being
through the Empress Maud there was no obstacle to her marriage,
afterwards effected, with Hamelin, the illegitimate son of Geoffrey
of Anjou.

so much more potent than the protests of Thomas the
Chancellor that the projected marriage had to be
abandoned. The young William took the matter so
much to heart that he retired to the court of his
mother, the empress, at Rouen, where he shortly
afterwards sickened and died on 30th January 1164.

Becket had deprived the king's clerks of their benefices, protected criminals from the king's justice,
opposed the king's financial schemes, and thwarted
the king's plans for his brother's advance. He had
also aggressively asserted the rights of Canterbury
against the Earl of Clare and others of the king's
barons and had excommunicated the king's tenant,
William of Eynesford, in a dispute over the advowson
of a church, the decision of which was claimed as
belonging to the king's court. Even if he had been
entirely in the right in every one of these questions
it would not have been extraordinary if the king, a
violently self-willed man, had become completely
estranged. And now the question of clerical immuni-
ties reached a climax. A long list of crimes committed
by clerks was presented to the king by his justices,
and one of these justices, Simon Fitz-Peter, made a
special complaint against Philip de Broi, a canon of
Bedford. The canon had been accused of the murder
of a knight and had cleared himself by his oath before
the Bishop of Lincoln, but Simon Fitz-Peter, who
was holding assizes at Dunstaple, apparently considering that the verdict of the ecclesiastical court
was contrary to evidence, ordered him to stand his

trial before himself ; Philip refused, and in course of argument used insulting expressions towards the justice, which the latter reported to the king. Henry, enraged at the insult to his representative, demanded that Philip should be retried on both charges, of murder and contempt of court, before a lay tribunal. This claim Becket successfully combated, and the king had to be content with a trial before an ecclesiastical court. The prelates who formed the court decided that the question of the murder had been finally disposed of by the acquittal before the Bishop of Lincoln and could not be re-opened, but for the insult to the king's officer they commanded that Philip de Broi should forfeit his prebend and go into exile for two years, and should also make a public apology to Simon Fitz-Peter clad in penitential garb. Henry declared that the sentence was absurdly light, and determined to bring the whole question of clerical and lay jurisdiction to a definite issue.

An opportunity soon offered, and at a council held at Westminster in October 1163, Henry definitely demanded that the bishops should swear to obey the ancient customs of the realm, which, he claimed, allowed a clerk to be indicted before a lay tribunal, sent for trial to the ecclesiastical court, and, if found guilty, degraded and, being no longer a clerk, sent back to the lay court to receive sentence. There was no question of trying clerks before lay judges, but the bishops, headed by Becket, took up the line that the Church's sentence must of necessity be just,

HENRY II DISPUTING WITH BECKET
(From Cott. M.S. Claud. Dii)

and that to inflict a further punishment after degradation would be to punish a man twice for one offence ;
they would therefore only consent to the " ancient
customs," of which they denied the antiquity and
legality, " saving the rights of their order," or in
other words reserving the liberty to interpret them
as they pleased. The king at once broke up the
council, deprived Becket of the custody of the honours
of Eye and Berkhamstead, and withdrew the young
Prince Henry from his care. An interview between
the king and the archbishop outside Northampton
did not mend affairs, but by the advice of Arnulf,
Bishop of Lisieux, Henry adopted the policy of
detaching the bishops from Becket and gradually
isolating him. Bishop Hilary of Chichester had
from the first been willing to accept the customs,
and Gilbert Foliot of London, and Roger, Archbishop
of York, lent their aid, more from dislike of the
primate than from approval of the king's schemes.
Finding himself almost unsupported the archbishop
listened to the arguments of the papal nuncio, Philip,
Abbot of Aumône, and Robert of Melun, Bishop-elect
of Hereford, and agreed to withdraw the obnoxious
reservation and accept the customs. Not content
with the verbal promise thus made before him at
Oxford, Henry determined to have the acceptance
of the customs formally and publicly ratified, and
accordingly he summoned a great council to meet
at Clarendon in January 1164.

At this Council of Clarendon were present the

E

peers, both spiritual and lay, in full force; the Earls of Cornwall, Leicester, Hertford, Essex and Chester, Arundel, Salisbury and Ferrers; the Counts of Brittany and Eu; Richard de Lucy, the justiciar; Richer of l'Aigle, Becket's old patron; Simon Fitz-Peter, the insulted justice, and the representatives of such great families as Bohun, Mowbray, Braose, Warenne, Cheyney, Beauchamp, and Dunstanville, all of whom gave their assent to the code of laws now presented on the king's behalf as embodying the customs of the realm concerning the Church prevalent in the time of his grandfather, Henry I. The prelates had apparently expected that they would be called upon to promise obedience to certain vague and undefined " ancient customs," which could be subsequently eluded by denying that any particular regulation which infringed their privileges rightly belonged to that category. When they heard the very definite and exact claims advanced by the Crown they met the demand for their assent with an absolute and united refusal, as was indeed to be expected.

The details of these Constitutions of Clarendon will be discussed elsewhere, but the main points were, briefly, as follows. The claim, already referred to, that clerks might be accused before a lay judge, and if condemned and degraded by the ecclesiastical court, the proceedings in which were to be watched by one of the king's justices, might be sentenced as laymen. That appeals might be made from the bishop's court to that of the archbishop and from

the latter to the king, without whose leave no appeal
should be made to the Pope; to strengthen this
latter provision it was ordained that no ecclesiastic
should leave the kingdom without the royal licence.
That no tenant-in-chief should be excommunicated
or his lands interdicted without the king's leave;
that pleas touching advowsons should belong to the
king's courts; and that the sons of villeins should
not be ordained without the permission of their
lords. Becket, as leader of the Church party, rejected the customs completely. He reasserted the
finality of sentences passed in ecclesiastical courts,
and declared that the proposed sentencing of the
condemned clerk by the lay court would be "to
bring Christ before Pilate a second time." The prohibition of papal appeals he denounced as contrary
to the consecration oaths of the bishops, by which
they were bound to allow such appeals, and the
restriction on the passage of the clergy across the
seas he declared would place them in a position of
inferiority as compared with laymen and would discourage pious pilgrimages. Finally, on the whole
question he took up the uncompromising attitude that
the Church was the giver of laws and the ruler of
kings, and that human laws which interfered with
its privileges were of no effect.

Negotiations were opened on the king's behalf by
the Bishops of Norwich and Salisbury, who pointed
out to Becket the probable consequences for all the
prelates of inflaming the king's anger, which con-

sequences they themselves would be the first to feel, as they were out of favour with Henry. Their representations proving of no effect, the Earls of Cornwall and Leicester besought him to consider the difficult position in which they and other peers, faithful sons of the Church, would be placed if the king persisted in his demands to the point of ordering the arrest and trial of the archbishop. Finding him obdurate they withdrew, and the next attempt at effecting a compromise was made by two knights of the Order of the Temple, Richard de Hastings, the English Grand Master, and Otes de St. Omer. Combining in themselves the attributes of knights and ecclesiastics, they were well suited to act as arbitrators, and their arguments appear to have had some effect ; so that when at last the impatient crowds of courtiers began to threaten and show signs of violence, the wearied archbishop broke down under the strain and condescended to an unworthy act of casuistry. Turning to his astonished fellow prelates he exclaimed, " If the king insists upon my perjuring myself I must do so, and must hope to purge the sin by future penance." Proceeding to the king's council chamber he declared his acceptance of the customs, " honestly, in good faith and without deceit," and at his command the bishops also signified their consent. Henry at once demanded that Becket should swear to observe the customs, and should affix his seal to a written copy thereof. To the first demand Becket replied that a priest's word was as good as an

oath, while the question of sealing he managed to
waive for the time being, accepting a copy of the
customs by way of protest. Following up his victory,
Henry caused both archbishops, of Canterbury and
York, to write to the pope desiring him to confirm
the customs. This they did, to please the king,
knowing well that the pope would refuse to sanction
any such infringement of the Church's privileges.
At the same time Henry desired the pope to appoint
the Archbishop of York legate for all England.
Alexander, while refusing to confirm the customs,
granted the legation to Archbishop Roger, but by
exempting Becket and the church of Canterbury
deprived the grant of its point. Henry indignantly
returned the letters of legation and refused a further
offer of the legation for himself.

Becket left Clarendon deeply humiliated at his
own weakness, and even went so far as to suspend
himself from the performance of divine service for a
time. A letter to the pope explaining and lamenting
his action received a sympathetic reply virtually absolving him from the promise which he had made
but had never intended to keep. Not content with
this, however, he determined to visit the papal court,
at this time established at Sens, in person, and actually set sail from Romney with that intention, but
was foiled in his attempt to cross the Channel by
contrary winds, coupled with the boatmen's fear of
incurring the king's anger. This infringement of
one of the articles of the Clarendon Constitutions was

reported to Henry, and served to embitter him yet
more against Becket and to precipitate the crisis
which now arose. One of the king's officers, John
the Marshal, having brought an action in the archbishop's court touching an estate held of the manor
of Pagham in Sussex, being defeated in his claim
availed himself of the section in the Constitutions
which permitted an appeal to the king, and made such
an appeal, taking oath that justice had not been done
to him. The archbishop was accordingly ordered to
attend and answer the plea at Westminster on 14th
September 1164. On that day Becket was unwell,
and sent four knights with letters from himself and
from the sheriff of Kent testifying that he was ill,
and alleging that John's case ought to be set aside
as he had deceitfully sworn upon a tropiary, or
hymn-book, instead of upon the Gospels. The king
vowed that Becket's plea of illness was false, stormed
at the knights, refused to listen to them, and named
a fresh day, 6th October, for hearing the suit at
Northampton. By this time the breach between the
once inseparable friends had so widened that the
king would not send even formal documents direct
to the archbishop, as to do so would involve addressing
him with a polite formula of salutation which was
very far from expressing his real feelings. For the
council to be held at Northampton, therefore, Becket,
instead of receiving the personal summons due to
his. rank, was summoned through the sheriff, and

when he greeted the king at Northampton he was refused the kiss of welcome.

John the Marshal was absent on the king's business at the Exchequer on the first day of the council, but next day he duly appeared in court, and Becket was ready to answer him. Henry, however, swept aside Becket's arguments and pleadings, accused him of contempt of court for not having appeared in person on the previous occasion, and demanded sentence against him. The court, fearing the king and considering that Becket had been guilty of contempt, condemned him to be " at the king's mercy." Theoretically this meant that he forfeited all his chattels to the king, but in practice the forfeiture was commutable for a fixed sum, which varied in different parts of the country : for a citizen of London the fine was a hundred shillings, for a man of the privileged county of Kent only forty shillings. In this case, however, the court arbitrarily departed from the established custom and pronounced sentence of complete forfeiture. To decide on the verdict was one thing, to pronounce sentence against the head of the English Church was another ; the barons declined to do so, and said it was clearly a task for the spiritual peers ; the latter retorted that they could not be expected to sentence their own head ; but finally by the king's order sentence was pronounced by the aged Bishop Henry of Winchester, a thorough supporter of Becket's ecclesiastical policy. Hardly

had this been done when Henry demanded of the
archbishop an account of three hundred pounds owing
for the honours of Eye and Berkhamstead which he
had held of the king's grant. Thomas very rightly
replied that he had had no notice of any such demand,
and further stated that he had laid out the whole
amount, and more, in building operations on the
king's behalf. So far as Berkhamstead is concerned,
the Pipe Rolls seem to show that all arrears due to
the king had been paid the previous year ; but as
the honour of Eye was not accounted for while
Becket held it as chancellor, it is possible that there
might have been some foundation for the claim,
though nothing could justify the way in which it
was advanced. Whatever the rights of the case the
verdict was, of course, against Becket, and when he
protested against the indignity of being called upon
to find sureties for payment he was told that his goods
having been declared forfeit he was no longer a man
of substance. Accordingly, the Archdeacon of Canterbury became his surety for one hundred pounds, and
the Earl of Gloucester, the Count of Eu, and William
of Eynesford for one hundred marks apiece.[1]

Next day Henry renewed his attack upon the
same lines, demanding back five hundred marks
which he had lent Thomas as chancellor at the time
of the Toulouse expedition, and calling for an account
of all the issues of vacant sees and abbeys which had

---

[1] Their names occur as owing these sums " pro plegio archi-
episcopi " on the Pipe Roll, 11 Henry II.

been in his custody during the period of his chancellorship. The king's intention of breaking the
archbishop by fair means or foul was now so clear that
the time-serving lords who had till lately been proud
to pay court to Becket now avoided him; his old
friend and supporter the Bishop of Winchester ad-
vised him to resign his see, and Hilary of Chichester
urged the same course, which other counsellors as
strongly discountenanced. Worn out by the strain,
Becket fell ill and was unable to appear in court on
the sixth day, Monday, 12th October; Henry again
disbelieved his excuse, and sent a number of barons
to see him and report. Thomas undertook to come
next morning even if he had to be carried in a litter.
He now determined to bring matters to a crisis and
prepared to face the worst. His preparations were
significant, if somewhat theatrical. Early in the
morning he went into the chapel of St. Andrew's
Priory, where he was lodging, and going to the altar
of St. Stephen celebrated the mass of the proto-
martyr. After this his intention had been to proceed to the court in full canonicals, barefooted and
carrying his own cross; from such an ostentatious
defiance to the king to do his worst his friends managed to dissuade him, and he rode in the usual way
to the castle. But when he had dismounted at the
entrance to the hall he took the processional cross
from the hands of Alexander Llewellyn, his Welsh
cross-bearer, and insisted upon carrying it himself.
Such a plain challenge to the king, signifying his

appeal to the protection of the Cross from the royal
injustice and violence, horrified his followers. The
Archdeacon of Lisieux besought the Bishop of London
to prevent it; Foliot replied, " My good friend, he
always was a fool and always will be ! " Nevertheless he attempted to dissuade the archbishop from
his fatal course, claiming the right to carry the cross
himself, as Dean of Canterbury, and even endeavouring to wrest it from Becket by force. Finding his
efforts of no avail he desisted, contenting himself
with the remark that if the king now drew his sword
they would make a fine pair. Becket then entered
and seated himself apart, holding his cross and
attended by Herbert of Bosham and William Fitz-
Stephen. Meanwhile the bishops had been called
in to speak with the king, and Becket's old enemy,
Roger, Archbishop of York, had availed himself of
the opportunity to insult his fallen rival by having
his archiepiscopal cross carried before him, a deliberate infringement of the privileges of the see of
Canterbury, within whose province Northampton lay.[1]
While the course that events would take was still uncertain, Becket's attendants were giving him very
contradictory advice : Herbert of Bosham, the fiery
theologian, counselled him to hurl the thunders of
excommunication against his enemies if they dared
to offer violence to his person, but the cautious and

---

[1] The claim of the northern archbishops to have their cross carried
before them within the province of Canterbury was a continual
source of dispute for several centuries, leading to many undignified
scenes.

level-headed lawyer, William Fitz-Stephen, depre-
cated such a course and urged him to imitate the
saints of old and suffer wrong with meekness and
patience.

The archbishop having inhibited the bishops from
sitting in judgment upon him for any plea touching
matters prior to his consecration, and having also
appealed to Rome against the excessive and unprecedented sentence of forfeiture, Gilbert Foliot at once
lodged a counter appeal and Bishop Hilary of
Chichester protested against Becket's breach of the
Constitutions, which he, and at his suggestion all the
bishops, had so recently promised on their priestly
word to obey " honestly, in good faith and without
deceit." Becket's defence was to the effect that
the very qualifying words which Hilary quoted
justified his action, for nothing could be observed
in good faith that was contrary to the Christian
faith, or honestly which was against the Church's
honour ; adding that if they had shown weakness at
Clarendon it was the more necessary that they should
be strong now. Finding all hope of compromise gone,
the king sent the Earl of Leicester to pronounce sentence upon the archbishop. The sentence would
most probably have involved imprisonment, but it
was never pronounced, for Becket indignantly ordered
the earl to desist from uttering sentence against his
spiritual father, further declaring with justice that
he had been summoned to answer only in the case of
John the Marshal and could not be called upon to

account for all his doings as chancellor without summons, especially as at the time of his consecration the king's ministers had expressly undertaken that he should not be called to account for any of his acts as chancellor.

The earl retired abashed, and after a decent interval Becket rose and, still carrying his cross, left the hall. As he went he stumbled against a faggot, and Randulf de Broc cried out that he stumbled like the traitor that he was. The taunt of traitor was taken up and repeated in particular by Hamelin, the king's illegitimate brother, now Earl of Surrey and Warenne by his marriage with the Countess Isabel. Turning angrily on the earl, Becket exclaimed, " If it were not for my cloth I would show you whether I am a traitor or not ! " The clamour reached the king's ears, and he at once sent a messenger to proclaim that no one was to insult or molest the archbishop. He accordingly reached his quarters at St. Andrew's safely, and while seated at supper meditating upon his further course of action he received an omen which confirmed the intention, already half formed in his mind, of flight, for in the evening lection occurred the passage, " If men persecute you in one city, flee unto another." As he heard this phrase read out, Thomas looked across significantly at Herbert of Bosham, and as soon as he had an opportunity of speaking to him in private he bade him hasten to Canterbury, obtain as much money as possible from the archiepiscopal estates, and then cross to the monas-

tery of St. Bertin at St. Omer and await his coming.
Then he expressed his intention of keeping vigil
throughout the night in the church, refusing the
proffered company of the monks; and a little before
daybreak he stole away in disguise under the guidance
of a canon of Sempringham, with only two other
companions.

When Henry heard next morning of the archbishop's flight he sent orders to Dover and other
ports to prevent his crossing, and then turned with
some relief to the business of the approaching expedition against the Welsh. Meanwhile Thomas, knowing that search would be made for him in Kent, had
turned north, reaching Grantham on the first day,
and then on to Lincoln, where he stayed at the house
of a fuller. From Lincoln he went by water to
Sempringham Priory and so to Boston. Probably
finding that that port was watched, he turned south,
and after visiting Haverholme proceeded by unfre-
quented paths into Kent, travelling chiefly at night,
and for a week lay hidden at Eastry, until on the
evening of 2nd November circumstances enabled him
to set sail. After a rough voyage he landed in
Flanders near Gravelines; but he was not yet in
safety, for Henry, whose embassy to the papal court
had just crossed the Channel, had warned the Count
of Flanders of the possibility of Becket's landing in
his territory, and the count bore the archbishop ill-
will for the opposition which he had offered to the
marriage of the Abbess Mary of Boulogne to the

count's brother. Worn out by the hardships of the
sea voyage Thomas found himself unable to walk,
and the only means of conveyance obtainable proved
to be a pack-horse. Laying their garments in place
of the lacking saddle his companions lifted the weary
archbishop on to the horse, and in this humble guise
he, whose gorgeous cavalcade had once been a nine
days' wonder, entered Gravelines. Yet, though in
poor dress, treated by his companions with a careful
absence of ceremony and passing as " Brother Christian," there were little distinctions between him and
his friends which nothing could efface, and which
did not escape the notice of the innkeeper at whose
house he put up. The man and his servant, who also
recognised the archbishop, proved honest, and Thomas
safely accomplished the remainder of his journey to
St. Omer. Here he met not only his faithful Herbert
of Bosham but also the justiciar, Richard de Luci.
The justiciar having vainly endeavoured to persuade Becket to return to England, promising him
his own good services with the king, formally renounced all allegiance to him and departed.

To follow the course of the struggle between king
and archbishop during the six years of Becket's exile
in detail is a wearisome and unprofitable task. Constant efforts at mediation, incessant appeals and
counter-appeals to Rome, broadcast excommunica-
tions involving the most prominent men at Henry's
court and all who had dealings with them, till hardly
a person of eminence stood outside the Church's ban,

mutual recriminations, and anything and everything
except reason and compromise. The king's absolute
insistence upon the Constitutions of Clarendon was
met by Becket with a blank refusal. So far as we
can judge Henry might have been persuaded to
accept a compromise had the archbishop shown the
least inclination to meet him half-way, and such a
course would certainly have had powerful support
from the wiser and more temperate royal officers.
As it was, it is remarkable that, while a considerable number of prominent ecclesiastics were in opposition to Becket, he does not seem to have had
the support of a single English or Norman layman
of any eminence.

Henry, in a moment of anger at Becket's flight,
had sent an imperious letter to King Louis demanding
the return of Thomas, " late Archbishop of Canterbury " ; Louis inquired, with some justice, who had
deposed the archbishop, adding that he in his kingdom could not displace the meanest clerk ; the
request for the return of Thomas he refused, going
out of his way to offer the fugitive cordial hospitality.
Henry's embassy to the pope at Sens, consisting of
the Archbishop of York, the Bishops of Chichester,
London, and Worcester, the Earl of Arundel and
others, met with equal unsuccess. The archbishop
and the Bishops of London and Chichester all spoke
with great vehemence against Becket, but the papal
court was more amused at certain slips of accent
and construction in their Latin than convinced by

their argument, and it was only the calm and reasoned speech of the Earl of Arundel, who spoke in his native French, that produced any impression. The pope refused to do anything until Becket had come to state his own case, and the embassy, having strict orders to return at once, withdrew. Thomas on his arrival produced his copy of the Constitutions, which the pope had not previously seen. They were, naturally, declared to be intolerable infringements of the rights of the Church and St. Peter, and the pope sternly rebuked Thomas for ever having given his consent to them. At this time, apparently, Becket surrendered the primacy into the pope's hands, receiving it back again from him. By so doing he was not only confirmed in full possession of the see but was in the position to deny that he owed his archbishopric to the king. Pope Alexander was now very awkwardly placed, for while his position as head of the Church compelled him to uphold Becket, his recognition as pope had been largely due to Henry's support, and if that support were withdrawn and given to the schismatic antipope, Alexander's hold on the papacy would be dangerously weakened. The reality of this danger was soon made clear, when, in May 1165, Henry's ambassadors, Richard of Ilchester, Archdeacon of Poictiers, and John of Oxford, who were present at the Emperor Frederic's council at Wurzburg nominally on business touching the proposed marriage of Henry's daughter Maud, virtually pledged their royal master to support the emperor and the antipope against Alexander. Feeling, however, ran too strongly against Henry in this matter, and he had to repudiate the action of his ambassadors.

The pope, cautiously avoiding a complete breach with Henry, declared that certain of the Constitutions were quite inadmissible but that others were tolerable, and, by refraining from any definite pronouncement as to any particular sections, left an opening for negotiations. At the same time he attempted to bring the king to reason through the mediation of the Bishops of London and Hereford, Archbishop Rotrou of Rouen, and the Empress Maud. But matters had already gone too far for any friendly arrangement to be possible. Becket, who after his interview with the pope had established himself, in December 1164, at the Cistercian abbey of Pontigny, was determined to yield nothing, and had already commenced the campaign of letters, argumentative, mandatory, supplicatory and threatening, with which he disturbed the peace of Western Europe for the next five years; and Henry, at his Christmas council at Marlborough, had retorted by confiscating the property of the see of Canterbury. Not content with this legitimate seizure of the archbishop's revenues, the king extended his attack to all persons connected with Becket by family or official ties, and all his poor relations and such of his clerks as had proved themselves faithful to his cause were stripped of their possessions and sent into exile

F

under a vow to join their patron. This step, designed to worry Becket and to strain his already
straitened finances, seems to have owed its full
rigour if not its inception to Ranulf de Broc, into
whose hands the property of the see had been committed, and was opposed by Bishop Hilary of
Chichester on the ground that, while so manifestly
unjust an act would put the king in the wrong, the
chief effect would be to strengthen Becket by surrounding him with a crowd of faithful servants.

During the year 1165 little worthy of note occurred,
but with the spring of 1166 Becket began to adopt
more vigorous measures. Assured in his own mind
of the support of the pope, who on 24th April appointed the archbishop Legate of England, Thomas
wrote three successive letters to King Henry, couched
in language of increasing severity, warning and
threatening him. The king, who was at Chinon,
could only tie Becket's hands by an appeal to Rome
against his threatened action, and accordingly sent
the Bishops of Séez and Lisieux to Pontigny to give
notice of his appeal. On their arrival at Pontigny
on Ascension Day, 2nd June, they found that Thomas
had gone to Soissons to visit the shrine of St.
Drausius, a favourite resort of persons about to
fight a judicial duel. Invigorated by his visit to the
combative saint, Becket went on to the abbey of
Vézelay, and on Whitsunday, 22nd June, to the
astonishment and dismay of his unsuspecting companions, publicly excommunicated Richard de Luci

and Joscelin de Bailliol as authors of the Clarendon Constitutions, Richard of Ilchester and John of Oxford for taking part with the schismatics at Wurzburg, John of Oxford being further condemned for accepting the Deanery of Salisbury in spite of prohibition, and Randulf de Broc and others for usurping the possessions of the church of Canterbury, while the king himself was threatened with a similar fate. The sentences created little excitement outside the circle of Becket's own audience; most of those against whom they were fulminated were becoming seasoned to excommunication, and the king was sustained by the comfortable knowledge that the pope would support him. In the previous May Henry had given orders for a levy throughout his dominions on behalf of the Crusade, and some months earlier he had shown further evidence of his zeal for the Church by presiding at Oxford over a council which condemned a little band of German or Flemish heretics who had settled in England. These heretics, humble weavers under the leadership of one Gerard, seem to have held opinions similar to those of the Waldensian Protestants; they met with little or no success in their missionary efforts, and, having refused to recant, were branded and scourged and turned out into the snow, to perish of cold and hunger. Fortified with the knowledge of his good services to the Church, Henry did not even hesitate to appoint the excommunicate John of Oxford as envoy, with John Cumin and Ralph of

Tamworth, to the papal court. On their arrival Pope Alexander gave them a friendly welcome, absolved John of Oxford and confirmed him in possession of the Deanery of Salisbury, quashed Becket's sentences and ordered him to refrain from molesting the king, at the same time promising to appoint commissioners to arbitrate between the king and the archbishop.

Towards the end of the year 1166 Henry had been successful in procuring Becket's removal from Pontigny by threats against the Cistercian order. His star was distinctly in the ascendant, and he could afford to await with equanimity the long-delayed arrival of the papal commissioners, the cardinals Otto and William of Pavia. Becket, on the other hand, was angered by the pope's action and especially by the appointment of Cardinal William, and expressed himself with a vehemence which even his friend John of Salisbury considered excessive. The enormous mass of correspondence concerned with the Becket controversy which has been preserved is throughout remarkable rather for vigour than elegance. In letters which are a mosaic of quotations and reminiscences from the Vulgate, with an occasional phrase from a classical poet, the writer's adversaries are compared to the most notorious villains of Scripture, while contempt is poured on them by means of sarcastic puns, Richard de Luci, the great justiciar, becoming " Luscus "—the one-eyed or half-blind—and the Archdeacon of Canterbury

figuring as the "archdemon." The whole correspondence breathes a spirit of intolerance which
augured ill for the efforts of would-be mediators.
Of these mediators the one of whom most might
have been hoped, Henry's mother, the Empress
Maud, died at Rouen on 10th September 1167. As a
devoted daughter of the Church she had condemned
the excessive severity of her son's anti-clerical
legislation, though as "a daughter of tyrants" she
had approved the general trend of the Clarendon
Constitutions. Her influence with Henry was great,
and if compromise had been possible it would no
doubt have been exerted to that end, but, as it was,
she could do nothing beyond such moderating
measures as interfering on behalf of an imprisoned
and tortured bearer of papal letters.

When the papal legates at last opened negotiations
in November 1167, by an interview with the archbishop at Planches on the borders of France and
Normandy, they found him resolute to agree to
nothing without the addition of the disputed phrase
"saving the liberty of the Church," and all their
arguments were useless. When they made their
report to Henry he dismissed them angrily with some
uncomplimentary remarks on the subject of cardinals.
A renewed appeal by the English bishops tied
Beckct's hands till November 1168, and in May of
that year the pope remonstrated with him and
ordered him to take no action against the king until
the beginning of Lent, 5th March 1169. At the

same time Alexander made an effort to bring matters to a settlement by appointing two monks, the Prior of Mont Dieu and Simon de Coudre of Grammont, as commissioners. They did not act until 7th January 1169, when Henry and Louis met at Montmirail to negotiate a treaty. Becket was with the French king, and when the commissioners had presented to Henry a letter from the pope urging him to a speedy reconciliation, the archbishop came forward with every appearance of humility and expressed his desire for peace. Henry was willing to receive him back into favour if he would undertake to act loyally, but Becket would only pledge himself to obedience " saving the honour of God," or in other words " the liberty of the Church." In vain Henry offered him every right and possession that his predecessors in the see of Canterbury had held, provided that he would obey the laws that they, many of them saints, had obeyed. A suggestion that Thomas should return to his post without any definite mention being made of the Constitutions, with a tacit understanding that the more objectionable sections should be modified, was also rejected, and the conference broke up.

Shortly after this the commissioners presented to Henry letters from the pope couched in stern language and warning him of the consequences if he did not soon come to terms with Becket. Nevertheless Alexander was not prepared to take extreme measures, and accordingly he appointed yet other mediators, the Cardinals Gratian and Vivian, and wrote to Becket ordering him to take no action against the king or his supporters until they had performed their mission. Before this order reached the archbishop at Sens, where he had fixed his headquarters since his expulsion from Pontigny, he had availed himself of the expiration of the term of inaction previously set him, and early in March excommunicated the Bishop of Salisbury, Earl Hugh of Norfolk, and other offenders, laymen and clerks, following this up on Palm Sunday, 13th April, with the excommunication of the Bishop of London and the announcement of a similar fate in store for Geoffrey Ridel, archdeacon of Canterbury, Richard of Ilchester, Richard de Luci, and others. Anticipating his action the two bishops had already made provisional appeals to the pope, while precautions were taken to prevent the delivery of the notice of excommunication. But on Ascension Day, 29th May, during the celebration of mass in St. Paul's, a young Frenchman, Berenger by name, under pretence of making an oblation, handed to the priest celebrant the archbishop's letters, charging him to deliver them to the Bishop of London and publicly denouncing the latter excommunicate. Bishop Foliot, while accepting the sentence as valid, renewed his appeal to the pope, who strongly disapproved of Becket's action and ordered him to suspend his sentences until the nuncios had seen the king.

Gratian and Vivian reached Damfront on 23rd

August, and next day had an interview with the
king, in which he endeavoured to dictate to them,
insisting that the excommunicates should be absolved at once. For a week no progress was made,
but on 31st August, at Bayeux, Henry undertook
that if the excommunicates were absolved at once
he would receive back the archbishop and his friends
and allow him to hold his church and former possessions " to the honour of God, of the Church, of
the king and of the king's sons." Next day, however, he insisted upon the further significant addition
of the phrase " saving the dignity of my realm."
Even to get so far as this had proved a difficult task.
The meeting had been held in the open air, and twice
Henry had mounted his horse and turned to ride off in
a rage, expressing his contempt for the nuncios and
their threats of excommunication and interdict. A
proposal to counterbalance the " dignity of the
realm " with " the liberty of the Church " having
failed, negotiations were broken off. Becket, as
papal legate for England, having threatened to lay
England under the dread sentence of interdict, by
which all public services and religious ministrations
were suspended, Henry issued orders that the bearer
of such a sentence and any persons who obeyed it
should be held guilty of high treason, at the same
time prohibiting all monks and clergy from crossing
the seas without his leave, and ordering the search
of all laymen coming into England from foreign
countries. He further consented to another meeting

with the archbishop at Montmartre, whither he had gone to visit King Louis.

The negotiations at Montmartre in November 1169 turned chiefly upon the question of the restoration of Becket's estates. While the king was willing to restore him to the possession of what he held when he left the country, Thomas insisted upon full payment of all arrears, the surrender of certain disputed estates and the displacement of such clergy as had been presented by the king to Canterbury livings during his exile. Offers of arbitration were refused by Becket; and, while Henry consented that he should have all that his predecessors had on the same terms by which they held, his promise of due service to the king was qualified by the obnoxious phrase, "saving the honour of God." Henry therefore refused Becket the "kiss of peace," and the conference broke up. The terms offered by Henry appear to have made a favourable impression upon Pope Alexander, and he determined to make a final effort for a settlement on those lines. Accordingly, in the early spring of 1170, the Archbishop of Rouen and the Bishop of Nevers were appointed to negotiate; the Canterbury estates were to be restored in full, but the question of arrears might be waived; there was to be no reference to the Constitutions, and the kiss of peace was to be given by either the king or his son. If Henry refused to come to terms sentence of interdict should be laid upon his continental domains.

Negotiations remained for some little time in abeyance, as Henry had crossed to England, for the first time for four years, landing at Portsmouth on 3rd March, after a stormy passage during which at least one of his forty ships was lost. The chief matter necessitating the king's return to England was his intention of establishing the succession to the throne beyond all doubt by the coronation of his eldest son, Henry, now sixteen years old. The need for this coronation of the heir during his father's lifetime, for which precedents could be found on the Continent but not in England, is far from clear, and its ultimate results were to prove disastrous. The most immediate result was the creation of a fresh grievance for Becket. It would seem that the pope, willing to please Henry and not knowing that the right to crown kings was a privilege of the Archbishops of Canterbury, had granted permission for the Archbishop of York to crown the young Henry, or else such permission had been granted during the vacancy of Canterbury in 1162. When the news of the proposed coronation reached Becket he wrote letters to Archbishop Roger and the English bishops in general prohibiting them from officiating, and similar letters were sent by the pope ; but none of these appear to have been delivered, and on Sunday, 14th June, the younger Henry was crowned at Westminster by Archbishop Roger, the Bishops of London, Durham, Salisbury, and Rochester assisting. For some reason the young king's wife, Margaret,

SEAL OF THE "YOUNG KING" HENRY (†)

had not been crowned with him, although a royal
outfit had been provided for her,[1] and she had been
ordered to hold herself in readiness at Caen, where
the queen was in residence. The omission was
taken by Margaret's father, King Louis, as a deliberate
insult, and was possibly so intended; but it is far
more probable that Henry had intended her to be
crowned with her husband, but had been obliged to
hasten the coronation in order to avoid the publica-
tion of the prohibitory papal letters.

Returning to Normandy, Henry met the papal
commissioners at Falaise and agreed to accept the
terms which they proposed. They then had an
interview with Becket and persuaded him to come to
Fréteval, where the French and English kings were
to hold a conference. On 22nd July, therefore,
Thomas rode out to meet Henry. The king was in
an excellent temper, and as soon as he saw the archbishop he pressed forward, doffing his cap and salut-
ing him affectionately. The two then withdrew and
held a long private consultation. Becket began by
reproaching Henry for his action in regard to the
coronation. The king defended himself, pleading
historical precedents, which Becket rejected as un-
sound, and producing papal letters granting leave
for the Archbishop of York to crown the young
Henry; these letters, however, dated from 1162,
when, as we have seen, some such coronation was
mooted if not actually performed, and were issued

[1] See Pipe Roll, 16 Henry II.

during the vacancy of the see of Canterbury. In the end Henry promised to do justice in the matter, and added some ambiguous remarks to the effect that he would punish all who played either him or the archbishop false. No word was said about the Constitutions, but the king promised to restore to Becket all that he had held three months before the date of his exile and to receive him and his friends back into favour. Becket dismounted and knelt before the king, but the latter leapt from his horse, raised the archbishop and held his stirrup while he remounted. The two old friends, once more united, rode back together and announced the conclusion of peace, to the amazement of all; and even a passage of arms between the excommunicate Archdeacon of Canterbury and Becket, due to the latter's refusal to reciprocate the king's general amnesty by absolving the excommunicates, was not allowed to disturb the serenity of the atmosphere. The only cloud was the king's persistent refusal of the kiss of peace, based on the rash oath which he had sworn in the presence of the French that he would never give it. On this Henry was resolute, though he expressed his willingness to kiss " his mouth, and his hands, and his feet a hundred times " when he returned to England. So much importance did Becket attach to this symbolic act that he endeavoured to obtain the kiss by a ruse at Amboise in October. For this purpose he came to the chapel where Henry was going to hear mass, in the course of which service the king would be obliged to give the ceremonial kiss; but, warned by the much excommunicated Nigel de Sackville, Henry ordered the celebration of a mass for the dead, in which the ceremony of the *pax* is omitted.

About this time Henry wrote to the young king and the regency council in England announcing the conclusion of peace between himself and the archbishop, and ordering the restoration of the former possessions of the see and the holding of a judicial inquiry into the question of the honour of Saltwood. Early in November the king sent a message to Becket regretting that military affairs in Auvergne prevented his meeting him at Rouen, but urging him to delay his departure no longer, and appointing John of Oxford, Dean of Salisbury, to accompany him. Becket accordingly proceeded to Witsand, whence he was to cross to England. During the previous three months he had been busy corresponding with the pope, and had procured from him letters suspending and excommunicating the Archbishop of York, the bishops who had taken part with him, and the inevitable Archdeacon of Canterbury. The sentence against York, London, and Salisbury, Becket despatched from Witsand to Dover, where those prelates happened to be, before his own departure. At last, on 1st December 1170, the archbishop set sail, and, avoiding Dover, landed at Sandwich. Here he was met by Randulf de Broc, Reynold de Warenne, and Gervase of Cornhill, sheriff of Kent. Their threats of violence were restrained by John of Oxford, and after reproaching the archbishop for coming into the realm with fire and sword they suffered him to proceed to Canterbury, where he was joyfully welcomed by the clergy and populace.

The messengers whom he had sent over after the conclusion of peace between himself and the king had warned him that the estates of the see had been plundered, and their appeal to the royal officers for the promised restoration of property had been postponed long enough to enable the actual holders to secure the rents payable at Michaelmas. Becket now found that most of the Christmas rents had been anticipated, and the manors so thoroughly pillaged that nothing but empty barns and ruinous houses remained. He had, however, other matters to occupy his mind : the representatives of the censured prelates came to him desiring him to absolve their masters. So far as Archbishop Roger was concerned Becket professed inability, the pope having reserved his case to himself, but he was ready to absolve the Bishops of London and Salisbury, conditionally on their undertaking to submit to the pope's demands. This they were willing to do, but they were dissuaded by Archbishop Roger, and all three went over to Normandy to make complaint to the king. Becket, anxious from personal affection as well as from policy to pay his respects to the young king, sent Richard, Prior of St. Martin's, to Winchester to announce his intention, and presented Henry with

three magnificent chargers gaily caparisoned. The
king, or rather his council, declined the archbishop's
proffered visit, but undeterred he started for Winchester, intending after his visit to the court to make
a tour of visitation throughout his province. The
first night he spent at Rochester and the next at
the Bishop of Winchester's house in Southwark, but
here he was met by Joscelin of Arundel, brother of
Queen Adelisa, who ordered him to return to Canterbury. This he did, taking with him a small escort
of some five or six men-at-arms. The existence of
this escort was magnified by his enemies into a
charge of riding about with a great army to capture
the king's castles, but it was certainly necessary,
for threats were being openly made against his life,
and the Brocs at Saltwood were indulging in a regular
campaign of outrage and insult. They seized his
wine, they hunted in his preserves, poached his
deer and stole his hounds, and as a culminating insult
cut off the tail of his pack-horse.

Becket was not a man to suffer insult patiently,
and on Christmas Day he preached in the cathedral,
and, after alluding to the probability of his murder,
delivered a furious denunciation of his enemies, and
excommunicated Robert de Broc and a number of
other offenders. The news of his action was at
once conveyed to King Henry, who was keeping
Christmas at Bur-le-Roi, near Bayeux. Infuriated
by this fresh breach of the peace, Henry uttered a
wild tirade against the upstart priest and against

his courtiers who sat idle and allowed their master to be insulted without avenging him. Four knights, William de Tracy, Hugh de Moreville, Reynold Fitz-Urse, and Richard le Breton, determined to gain the king's favour by the murder of the archbishop. Taking horse at once they made for the coast, and favoured by the wind reached Saltwood Castle on Monday, 28th December. Meanwhile Henry, while refusing to go so far as Engelger de Bohun and William Mauvoisin, who urged the archbishop's execution, had determined on his arrest. Richard de Humet was sent to England to Hugh de Gundeville and William Fitz-John, the young king's guardians, while Earl William de Mandeville and Saer de Quincy watched the continental ports in case Becket should try to escape. The four knights, openly proclaiming that the king had decreed Becket's death, collected a considerable force from the garrisons of the neighbouring castles, and on Tuesday, 29th December, rode into Canterbury. Failing to persuade the town authorities to assist them, they warned them not to interfere and rode on to the palace. Striding into the room where the archbishop and his attendants were sitting, the four knights, without a word of greeting, sat down in front of him. After a pause Reynold Fitz-Urse ordered him, in the king's name, to absolve the excommunicates and afterwards to stand his trial before the young king at Winchester. Before they delivered their ultimatum, Becket, understanding that they had a private message from the king, had caused his attendants to withdraw, but he now recalled them and delivered a calm and dignified reply justifying his action and explaining his position. To their threats he replied that the king had granted him his peace, but that in any case he would never yield or waver in his obedience to God and the pope for fear of death.

The knights had entered the archbishop's presence unarmed, and they now withdrew, uttering threats and defiance, to bring the argument of steel to bear where words had proved unavailing. The Brocs and others of their associates had seized the gate-house of the palace and placed it in charge of Simon de Crioill and William Fitz-Nigel, the archbishop's steward, who had joined the conspirators ; Becket's own esquire, Robert Legge, was forced by Reynold Fitz-Urse to assist in arming him, and one of the archbishop's knights, Ralph Morin, was placed under arrest. As the armed crowd pressed forward the great door of the archbishop's apartments was shut and bolted and for a moment they were foiled, but Robert de Broc knew the palace well, and, snatching up an axe left on the stairs by a workman, attacked a wooden partition that would give access to their victim's room. Hearing the crash and splintering of the woodwork the monks and clerks, powerless against the mail-clad assassins, seized Becket, and in spite of his protests and resistance hurried him by a private entrance into the church. Contrary

G

to his wishes the door was shut behind him, but
when the pursuers began to thunder upon it he insisted upon its being opened, that the church might
not seem to be turned into a fortress. The four
knights and their followers rushed in, headed by
Reynold Fitz-Urse, who flung down the axe with
which he had attacked the door and brandished his
sword. Hugh de Moreville faced the terrified people
clustered in the body of the church, while his comrades
searched for their victim. In the pillared gloom of
the dim evening Becket was not at first visible, and
he could easily have escaped into the darkness of the
crypt or by the neighbouring stairway to the safety
of the roof, but hearing cries of " Where is the traitor ?
Where is the archbishop ? " he stepped forward,
saying, " Here am I, no traitor but the priest of
God. And I marvel that you are come into the
church of God in such guise. What will ye with
me ? " To their threats of instant death he replied
by commending his soul to God, St. Mary, St.
Denis, and St. Elphage, and their endeavours to
drive or drag him out of the church he resisted with
all his strength, striking William Tracy a blow which
almost felled him to the ground. Tracy replied
with a cut at his head, but Edward Grim, one of
the only three clerks who had remained with their
master, intercepted the blow with his arm. Although
most of the force of the stroke was spent on Edward
Grim it drew blood from the archbishop's head.
A second blow, from Reynold's sword, drove Becket

THE MURDER OF BECKET
From Harl. MS. 5102)

to his knees, and with the third he fell with his arms stretched out towards the altar of St. Benedict. As he fell Richard le Breton struck him again with such violence that his sword broke upon the pavement, crying, " Take that for the love of my lord William, the king's brother," Richard having served the young William, whose early death was attributed to the foiling of his matrimonial schemes by Becket. As the assassins turned to leave the church, one Hugh Mauclerc, whose name is unknown to history save for this infamy, thrust his sword into Becket's gaping skull and scattered his brains upon the pavement. Thus fell Thomas Becket, the obstinate and imperious archbishop, and thus rose from his dead body Thomas of Canterbury, martyr and virtual patron saint of England.

Having wreaked their vengeance on the archbishop the murderers turned to the plunder of his palace. Everything of value they seized, sending off a parcel of papal bulls and similar documents to their royal master. Then they rode off, the four knights soon afterwards retiring to Moreville's castle of Knaresborough, while the Brocs remained at Saltwood, whence they threatened to return to Canterbury and outrage the martyr's body. Hearing of their threats the monks of Canterbury, by the advice of the Abbot of Boxley and the Prior of Dover, proceeded at once to bury the body, which, after lying for some time neglected during the panic which followed the murder, had been reverently placed before the high altar.

Accordingly the martyred archbishop was laid in a marble tomb in the crypt, clad in the penitential hair-shirt, which, to the surprise of all, he was found to have worn beneath his other garments, and in the vestments worn at the time of his ordination and preserved by him against his burial. The church having been polluted by bloodshed, Mass could not be said in it, and so without the rites and services of the Church were laid to rest the remains of him whose shrine was to be for future generations the great national centre of prayer and pilgrimage

CHAPTER VI

IRISH AFFAIRS

WHEN news of Becket's murder reached Henry at
Argentan on 1st January 1171, he was terribly per-
turbed, and, retiring to his apartments, remained for
three days in solitude, fasting and reviewing the
situation. It must have seemed at first as if the
officious knights by their rash action had wrecked his
whole policy. The murder was bound to alienate
many whose sympathy would otherwise have been
with the king; it would put a fresh weapon in the
hands of his enemies; and, above all, it would practically force the pope into that position of direct
antagonism which he had hitherto skilfully contrived
to evade. To extract himself from his position without complete loss of dignity and surrender of all for
which he had fought was a task worthy of Henry's
diplomatic genius. It was necessary to be cautious
but prompt, for his enemies were losing no time;
before Henry had resumed public life the Archbishop
of Sens, legate of France, King Louis and the Count
of Blois had all written to Pope Alexander denouncing Henry as the murderer, and three weeks later
the Archbishop of Sens had proclaimed an interdict
upon the king's continental dominions on the

strength of a papal letter addressed to himself and
the Archbishop of Rouen ordering such a course to
be adopted in the event of the arrest or imprisonment of the Archbishop of Canterbury. Against this
action the Archbishop of Rouen and the Bishops of
Worcester, Evreux, and Lisieux at once appealed,
and the interdict was temporarily suspended. About
the end of January, when the appellants and the
king's special envoys started for the papal court at
Frascati, news of the murder reached the pope.
Accordingly when Richard Barre, the Archdeacons
of Salisbury and Lisieux, and the other royal envoys
reached Frascati they could not at first obtain a
hearing, and it was generally believed that on
Maundy Thursday, 25th March, the pope would excommunicate Henry and lay England under interdict. The efforts of the envoys, however, backed
with the powerful argument of English gold, averted
this danger, and the dreaded day brought forth
only an excommunication of the actual murderers
and their abettors. A month later, after hearing the
appeal of the Bishops of Worcester and Evreux,
Pope Alexander confirmed the sentence of interdict
published by the Archbishop of Sens, but exempted
the king and gave orders for the absolution of the
Bishops of London and Salisbury. At the same time
he announced his intention of sending legates to
Henry to settle the terms of his absolution.

Henry meanwhile was preparing to carry into
effect the plan which he had had to abandon in 1155

for an invasion of Ireland.   The scheme possessed
several attractions.   To begin with, affairs in that
island really called for his active interference ;   there
was also the advantage that in Ireland he would
be more completely out of reach of any unwelcome
papal messengers than he would be in almost any
other spot in the civilised world ;   and finally, by
undertaking the reform of the Irish Church, which
had been urged upon him by Pope Adrian IV., he
would give to his expedition something of the nature
of a crusade and would earn the gratitude of the
pope.

Prior to 1166 Ireland had been practically exempt
from English interference and had settled its own
affairs by primitive methods of violence.   Resembling their nearest neighbours, the Welsh, in many
respects, the Irish were even more quarrelsome
and less advanced in the social scale.   Utterly
lacking in political unity, their score of kings and
princelets acknowledged the theoretical supremacy
of their Head King, or Ard-Righ, for just so long as
he could maintain his position by power of the battle-
axe.   The battle-axe, that excellent weapon for
quick-tempered men, doing its work with complete
finality in less time than a man can unsheathe sword
or notch arrow to bow, was the constant companion
of the Irishman and the arbiter of all his politics.
By a not unusual combination the Irish were at the
same time utter barbarians and consummate artists.
Their poetry was of a high standard; in music no

nation but the Welsh could compare with them;
and in metal work, carving, and painting such fragments as have come down to us show a complete
mastery of the beauties of line and colour. Commerce they left to the Scandinavian settlers along
their seaboard. Possessing a fertile soil and a
favourable climate they lacked the industry and
stability for agriculture, but grazed great quantities
of cattle, which served alike for the standard of
exchange, coined money not being in use, and for
the objective of raids during their incessant hostilities. When St. Patrick banished the reptiles
and vermin it would seem that they must have left
their venom and vice behind for the use of the inhabitants of the island, for never was there a race so
prone to anger, so ungrateful and so treacherous,
and even the miracles recorded of their saints were
more often concerned with vengeance wrought upon
sacrilegious offenders than with rewards bestowed
upon faithful devotees.

In this race of Ishmaelites there was one man of
evil pre-eminence whose hand was against all men
and all men's against him. Dermot MacMurrogh,
King of Leinster, since the beginning of his reign in
1121 had had even more than his share of fighting;
his voice had grown hoarse with the shouting of his
battle-cry; his borders had been enlarged at the
expense of his neighbours, and the envy and hatred
of rival chieftains had been incurred without gaining
him the affection of his own subjects. In 1152

IRISH WOMAN PLAYING A ZITHER

IRISHMEN ROWING IN A CORACLE
(From Royal MS. 13 B.viii)

he had carried off Dervorgille, the beautiful but
middle-aged wife of Tiernan O'Rourke, King of
Breifny ; as the lady was well past forty and Dermot
some ten years older the elopement would seem to
have been less a matter of romantic passion than
a studied insult to Tiernan. Dermot was speedily
forced by Turlogh O'Conor, then Ard-Righ, to give up
Dervorgille, but escaped for the time any serious
consequences. O'Rourke, however, did not forget,
and at last, in 1166, found an opportunity to head a
formidable combination against Dermot.   Finding
himself isolated Dermot seems to have looked to
England for help, for " the chancellor of the Irish
king " came to this country in 1100, and certain
Irishmen appear to have visited Henry's court at
Woodstock early in the same year.[1] No assistance
being obtained and resistance being impossible,
Dermot, with some sixty followers, crossed to England
and settled for a time at Bristol under the protection
of the wealthy Robert Fitz-Harding.

In the spring of 1167 Dermot crossed to Normandy
and had an interview with King Henry. The latter
had his hands too full to meddle with Irish affairs, but
the opportunity for getting some sort of footing in
Ireland which might be useful in the future was too
good to be missed ; he therefore took Dermot's
homage and issued a general licence in vague terms
encouraging any of his subjects to assist the exiled
king. With this Dermot returned to Bristol, and after

[1] See Pipe Roll, 12 Henry II.

vain attempts to obtain assistance in England
crossed into Wales, where he succeeded in interesting
Richard of Clare, Earl of Pembroke, in his cause.
The earl, whose extravagance had seriously impaired
his finances, was attracted by the hope of plunder and
broad lands and by the promise of Dermot's daughter
Eva in marriage, with the ultimate prospect of the
throne of Leinster ; he was, however, too cautious
to risk his English and Welsh estates by embarking
on this enterprise before he had obtained leave from
King Henry. Dermot therefore turned to King Rhys
of South Wales, who not only gave him a small force
of soldiers but undertook to allow his prisoner, Robert
Fitz-Stephen of Cardigan, to collect troops and cross
over to Ireland. At last Dermot landed in his country
once more with a small force, part of which was
commanded by Richard Fitz-Godebert of Pembrokeshire. After a little fighting Dermot came to terms
with his adversaries and dismissed his mercenaries.

For a short time Dermot remained quiet, but about
the end of 1168 he despatched his interpreter, Morice
Regan, to remind Robert Fitz-Stephen of his promise
and to obtain other assistance. Fitz-Stephen accordingly crossed to Ireland early in May 1169. With him
came Meiler Fitz-Henry, grandson of Henry I., and
Miles, son of the Bishop of St. David's, Maurice
Prendergast and Hervey de Montmorency, the needy
uncle of Earl Richard, and Robert de Barri, a nephew
of Fitz-Stephen and brother of the historian Gerald.
These adventurers landed with some three hundred

followers at Bannow near Wexford, and here they
were welcomed by Dermot and his son Donnell
Kavanagh. An assault on Wexford was repelled
with loss, but next day the city surrendered and was
granted to Fitz-Stephen. This success was followed
by an expedition against the King of Ossory, in
which the English, by skilful manœuvring, drew the
Irish out into open ground, where they were able
to use their cavalry with deadly effect ; the flying
natives were further punished by an ambuscade of
archers, and at the end of the day two hundred heads
were laid before Dermot for that savage king to
gloat upon. MacKelan of Offelan and O'Toole of
Glendalough were defeated and plundered, but
Roderic O'Conor, the Ard-Righ, was able to force
Dermot to acknowledge his supremacy and to surrender his son as hostage. Tired of the somewhat
unprofitable fighting, Maurice Prendergast and his
two hundred men proposed to return to Wales, but
Dermot refused to let them sail from Wexford.
Maurice at once transferred his services to the King
of Ossory and assisted his former enemy against his
former friends until such time as he discovered that
the jealous men of Ossory were plotting his destruction, when he withdrew his contingent secretly by
night to Waterford and thence crossed into Wales.

About the time that Maurice Prendergast left
Ireland Maurice Fitz-Gerald, a half-brother of Robert
Fitz-Stephen, had landed with some hundred and
forty soldiers, and not long afterwards, in the early

summer of 1170, the Earl of Pembroke obtained
leave from King Henry to undertake the Irish ad-
venture. He first sent a small force under the
redoubtable Raymond the Big, who threw up a
temporary fort at Dundonuil, where they had hard
work to defend themselves. By the ingenious device
of driving a herd of cattle before them the invaders
shattered the Irish ranks and, profiting by the confusion, slew many and captured seventy prisoners.
By the advice of Hervey de Montmorency the
prisoners were butchered, the business of beheading
them being entrusted to a bloodthirsty Welsh girl
whose lover had been killed in that battle. Shortly
afterwards Earl Richard landed with Maurice Prendergast, Miles de Cogan, and other barons and fifteen
hundred men. Two days later, on 25th August,
the attack on Waterford began, and its capture was
celebrated by the marriage of the earl and Eva,
daughter of King Dermot. The king and his English
allies next marched against Dublin, avoiding the
great host assembled against them under the Ard-
Righ on Clondalkin moor. The city was not prepared
to offer armed resistance, and the terms of surrender
were being discussed between Morice Regan, Dermot's
representative, and the saintly Archbishop Laurence
O'Toole and Hasculf Torkil's son, the Scandinavian
lord of Dublin, when suddenly, without warning,
Miles de Cogan, who had no intention of being deprived of his anticipated loot by the peaceful surrender of the city, raised his war cry and stormed the

walls. Hasculf and such of the inhabitants as were
fortunate enough to gain the ships escaped by water,
but very many were slain and the city was given over
to plunder. Miles was rewarded for his treacherous
act by the grant of the custody of the city, while
Earl Richard retired to Waterford and Dermot to
his capital at Ferns, where on 1st January, 1171,
he died

By the death of Dermot MacMurrogh, Earl
Richard became virtual King of Leinster. But the
success of the earl and his companion adventurers
was by no means a cause of satisfaction to King Henry,
who had no intention of allowing a warlike and independent kingdom to grow up so close to his own
realm. He accordingly made his feelings on this
subject obvious by seizing the Earl of Pembroke's
English estates, and the earl hastened to clear himself from the charge of disloyalty by sending his lieu-
tenant, Raymond the Big, to place all his conquests
at the king's disposal. Henry, who had gone so far
as to forbid the sending of any assistance in men or
munitions to Ireland and to order the immediate
return of the adventurers on pain of perpetual
banishment, was not appeased, though he determined
to profit by the earl's submission. Raymond seems
to have returned to his lord with an order for
the latter's personal appearance before the king.
Matters, however, were too involved to permit of
Earl Richard's immediate departure. Under pressure
from Archbishop Laurence O'Toole King Roderic

O'Conor had summoned a great force for the siege
of Dublin, and all the native chiefs had rallied round
him, glad of an opportunity of revenging the wrongs
they had suffered at the hands of the foreign invaders. Provisions soon began to fail in the city,
and an attempt to come to terms having failed, the
Ard-Righ insisting upon the surrender of all the
conquered territory except the three towns of Dublin,
Waterford, and Wexford, the only course open was
to risk all in an attack upon the besieging host.
The attempt might well seem desperate in view of
the disparity of numbers, but its very boldness
proved its salvation. Leaving a small garrison to
guard the city, some six hundred picked men marched
out in three columns, under Miles de Cogan, Raymond
the Big, and the earl himself. The surprise was
completely successful ; secure in the knowledge of
their numbers the Irish had neglected outposts or
guards and were caught quite unprepared ; many of
them were actually bathing when the English cavalry
dashed into their camp. Discouraged by this severe
defeat, in which they lost very heavily, the Irish
forces broke up and drifted away. Earl Richard was
now free to attempt the relief of Robert Fitz-Stephen,
who, after dangerously depleting his own forces to
strengthen the garrison of Dublin, had been gallantly
standing a siege in his castle of Carrick near Wexford.
The earl's forces, after a desperate action in the pass
of Odrone, in which Meiler Fitz-Henry particularly
distinguished himself, reached Wexford to find the

IRISH AXEMEN
(From Royal MS. B.viii)

town in flames, Carrick Castle fallen and Fitz-Stephen a prisoner. The earl now turned to Waterford and prepared for an expedition against MacDonnchadh, King of Ossory, but the latter offered to come in and make terms if his old ally Maurice Prendergast would obtain him a safe conduct. This Maurice did, but when MacDonnchadh came before the earl, King O'Brien of Munster, who was acting at this time with the English, urged his arrest and execution, and it was only by the vigorous action of Prendergast, who brought his men-at-arms on the scene, that the barons were prevented from thus treacherously breaking their oaths.

Leinster was now pacified and a further imperative summons from King Henry, already on his way towards Pembroke, necessitated the departure of Earl Richard. Hardly had he gone when Hasculf, the former lord of Dublin, landed with an army raised from Norway, the Isles, and Man, under the command of a man known from the berserk fury of his valour as John the Wode, or the Mad. These well-armed Scandinavians were foes of a different type from the wild Irish, but Miles de Cogan boldly charged upon them from the east gate, while his brother Richard, with a small force of thirty men-at-arms, rode secretly out of the west gate to take them in the rear. John the Wode, wielding his great axe with fearful effect, forced back the English, and had even gained footing within the gate when Richard's attack threw his men into confusion. Rallying his forces Miles charged

again upon the Northmen, who broke and fled;
John the Wode was killed fighting gallantly, and
Hasculf was captured and beheaded. Another as-
sault on the city, early in September, by the forces of
Tiernan O'Rourke, ended disastrously for the Irish,
and Dublin was left in peace.

Henry had landed at Portsmouth on 2nd August,
and after a visit to the aged Bishop Henry of Winchester, then on his deathbed, had marched towards
Bristol. At Newnham, in Gloucestershire, he was
met by Earl Richard, who surrendered to him the
cities of Dublin, Waterford, and Wexford, receiving
in return the royal favour and a grant in fee of the
residue of his conquests. About 8th September,
when the English army was approaching the borders
of Wales, King Rhys ap Gruffudd came to meet Henry
with the offer of a tribute of horses and oxen. This
tribute Henry soon afterwards respited, taking only
thirty-six horses as a token of friendship; at the
same time he restored to Rhys his son Howel, who
had long been held as hostage. Rhys showed his
appreciation of the king's friendship next year by
sending Howel to the English court to serve King
Henry. The peaceful passage of the English army
in Pembrokeshire, where the fleet was assembling
at Milford Haven, had been secured by this tactful
conciliation of King Rhys, and a troublesome chieftain,
Jorwerth ap Owain, was reduced to order by the
capture of his castle of Caerleon-on-Usk before Henry
reached Pembroke. For some three weeks the

English host lay weather-bound at Pembroke, part
of the time being spent by Henry in a pilgrimage to
St. David's, where he offered in the cathedral and
visited the bishop, David Fitz-Gerald. At last, on
16th October, the wind shifted and the fleet of some
two hundred vessels crossed over to Crook, near
Waterford. For a fortnight Henry remained at
Waterford, the government of which town he had
entrusted to Robert Fitz-Bernard. Here he received
the submission of the kings and chieftains of Ireland,
with the exception of the lords of Ulster and Roderic
O'Conor, the Ard-Righ. Hither also the men of
Wexford, in accordance with an undertaking given
to Henry at Pembroke by their envoys, brought
Robert Fitz-Stephen and his fellow-prisoners; and
Henry, whose personal intervention in Ireland had
been influenced in some degree by complaints of
the tyranny of some of the adventurers, thought it
politic to appease the natives by committing Robert
to prison for a short time. If he was mindful of the
demands of justice he was still more mindful of his
proposed reformation of the Irish Church, and having
received the homage of the Irish bishops he summoned
a council or synod at Cashel in November.

At this Council of Cashel canons were passed for
the observance of the degrees of affinity in marriage,
the performance of baptisms by priests in the church
—the local custom being for the father of the child
immediately after its birth to plunge it three times
into water, or into milk if the family were noble or

H

wealthy—the payment of tithes, and the immunity
of clerks and church property from secular exactions.
As soon as it was over Henry sent an account of the
proceedings, and of the submission tendered to him
by the bishops and princes of Ireland, to the pope by
the hands of the Archdeacon of Llandaff. It would
seem that he also endeavoured to obtain from
Alexander a confirmation of Pope Adrian's com-
mendatory letter issued in 1155, at the time when the
conquest of Ireland was first proposed. Alexander
did not grant this confirmation, but wrote letters to
Henry, to the bishops and to the kings of Ireland,
expressing his satisfaction at the steps taken to
remedy the monstrous irregularities of which the
Irish had been guilty, and his hope that Henry's
supremacy would make for the peace and better
government of the island. These letters must have
reached England some time in the summer of 1172.
Henry, however, does not seem to have been satisfied
with these expressions of papal approval ; possibly
he had in the first instance obtained the submission
of the Irish prelates by representing himself as
commissioned by Pope Alexander to reform their
Church ; however this may be, it would seem that
a synod was held at Waterford to which William
Fitz-Audelin brought probably Alexander's letters
and certainly the letter of Adrian (that famous
centre of controversy " the Bull *Laudabiliter*," so
called from its beginning with the word *Laudabiliter*
and, as befits an Irish document, its not being a

Bull),[1] and with it a confirmation by Pope Alexander, which was almost undoubtedly a forgery.

But before this synod of Waterford was held much had happened. Christmas in 1171 had been spent by the king at Dublin, where an elaborate palace, built of wattles in the native fashion, had been erected for him, and where the magnificence and luxury of his household, simple though it was if judged by continental standards, struck surprise into the minds of the Irish. But if the royal table presented a spectacle of unwonted luxury to the natives, the food of the country, the absence of wine, and the impurity of the water proved disastrous to the English. An exceptionally stormy winter aggravated the scarcity of provisions and consequent mortality, prevented operations against Roderic of Connaught, and by severing all connection with England left Henry a prey to unappeasable anxiety. Early in March 1172, news having possibly reached him of the arrival of the papal legates in Normandy, he moved down to Wexford, the greater part of his army going at the end of the month to Waterford; but for over six weeks the weather rendered the crossing to Wales impossible, and it was not till Easter Monday, 17th April, that Henry landed near St. David's, whence he made his way to Portsmouth, from which place he crossed to Normandy early in May.

[1] For a discussion of the authenticity of this letter of Pope Adrian, see Round, *The Commune of London*, 171–200, and, on the other side, Orpen, *Ireland under the Normans*, i. 312–8.

The arrival of the papal legates, coupled with
rumours of a conspiracy being formed by the young
King Henry and his brothers, had compelled Henry
to return from Ireland without attempting the sub-
jugation of the Ard-Righ and without strengthening
his hold upon the portions of the island already conquered by the erection of a series of castles. Before
leaving, however, he took measures intended apparently to weaken the power of the original adventurers alike for action independent of himself and
for the oppression of the natives. The government
of Dublin, with the province of Meath, he granted
to Hugh de Lacy, a man of character and ability,
who justified his selection by adopting a just and
conciliatory policy towards the Irish. With him
were associated in the charge of the city Robert Fitz-
Stephen and Meiler Fitz-Henry, while Waterford and
Wexford were committed to Robert Fitz-Bernard.
Earl Richard retained possession of Leinster, and was
apparently recognised as in control of the conquered
portion of Ireland; while the province of Ulster,
whose chiefs had refused to accept the English
supremacy, was handed over to John de Courcy to
subdue and enjoy as best he might.

The earl, who had made Kildare his chief seat,
had bestowed his daughter in marriage upon Robert
de Quency, whom he created hereditary constable of
Leinster; but not long after the marriage Robert
was killed in an expedition against O'Dempsey of
Offaly, leaving an infant daughter, who eventually

married the son of Maurice Prendergast. Raymond the Big then demanded the hand of the earl's widowed daughter, with the constableship, and upon his demand being refused retired into Wales. About the same time, in the summer of 1173, Henry, hard pressed by the rebellion of his sons, summoned some of the leading barons from Ireland, including Earl Richard, whom he made governor of Gisors. The appointment was of short duration, and the earl was soon invested with the government of Dublin, Waterford, and Wexford, and sent back to Ireland with letters recalling Hugh de Lacy, Fitz-Stephen, Fitz-Bernard, Prendergast, and others, who crossed at once, in time to take part in the battle at Fornham on 17th October 1173. The English forces in Ireland were thus seriously depleted, and an expedition led by the earl and Hervey de Montmorency into Munster having ended disastrously, all Ireland began to rise and endeavour to shake off the foreign yoke. Earl Richard hastily sent for Raymond, promising him the hand of his daughter, for which he had asked in vain before ; Raymond responded to the offer, landed with a small force at Waterford and marched to Wexford, where he reduced the town to order and obtained his coveted bride. Next year, in 1175, he led a force into Limerick and captured that town, but his successes, and possibly his excesses also, were displeasing to King Henry, and early in 1176 he was summoned to England to account for his actions. The state of affairs at Limerick, however, was too

desperate to permit of his absence, and after relieving
the garrison he thought it good policy to obtain a
renewal of their oaths of fealty to the king of England
from the kings of Connaught and Thomond. Raymond was therefore still in Ireland at the beginning
of June 1176, when Earl Richard died and William
Fitz-Audelin landed as procurator or justiciary of
Ireland.

Fitz-Audelin and his two coadjutors, Miles de
Cogan and Robert Fitz-Stephen, were recalled in 1177,
and Hugh de Lacy was appointed justiciary, Fitz-
Audelin being associated with Robert le Poer in the
custody of Waterford and Wexford, Miles and Robert
receiving South Munster, and North Munster, as yet
unsubdued, being granted to Philip de Braose,[1] from
which he got as little good as he deserved. For the
next seven years Henry left Ireland pretty much to
itself, and Lacy continued to strengthen the position
of the English settlement by building castles and by a
firm but conciliatory attitude towards the natives.
Unfortunately his success, coupled with his marriage
with a daughter of the king of Connaught, aroused
Henry's jealousy, and in 1184 he was removed from
office. As early as 1177 Henry had declared his
intention of making his young son John king of
Ireland, and in 1185 the furtherance of this design
afforded an excuse for keeping the beloved boy from

[1] This province had been previously offered to Herbert and
William Fitz-Herbert, half-brothers of Earl Reynold of Cornwall,
and Jolland de la Pomeray, but they had wisely declined the gift.

the distant dangers of the Crusade. John was at
this time in his nineteenth year, vain, pampered,
vicious, and as completely void of any redeeming
virtue as any young man could be. His father, to
whom he was as the apple of his eye, could hardly
have found in all his broad realms any person more
dangerously incompetent to undertake the difficult
government of Ireland.

On 31st March 1185, the king knighted his son at
Windsor, and almost immediately afterwards John
set out, under the charge of Ranulph de Glanville,
the justiciar, for Gloucester. After a few days' stay
in that city the heavy baggage and provisions for
the expedition, with the greater part of the forces,
were sent on to Bristol, while John himself with the
remainder passed on to Milford Haven, whence he
sailed for Waterford on 24th April. His force was of
imposing dimensions—it is said to have contained
three hundred knights—and as we find such men as
William le Poer and Stephen le Flemeng each bringing fifty horses, the total number of the cavalry must
have been large ; there was probably a contingent
of Flemish mercenaries, as Godescalk, " the master of
the Flemish serjeants," came from Kent, and there
must have been the usual proportions of archers and
foot soldiers. Significant is the entry on the Pipe
Rolls of payments for Roger Rastel and other huntsmen with horses and dogs who went from Somerset
into Ireland, and still more significant are the entries
of large sums spent in furnishing John's kitchen and

bakery. The bulk of John's followers were Norman
courtiers, despising their English companions, who
in turn regarded the Irish as despicable savages.
On John's arrival the friendly chieftains came to
welcome the son of the most powerful prince in
Christendom, but found an ill-mannered youth surrounded by a crowd of fashionable effeminate
flatterers. The Normans mocked at the barbaric
dress of the native princes, and carried their ill-bred
insolence so far as to pluck them by their long beards.
In justifiable anger the princes left the court at
Waterford and went to warn their compatriots of
the treatment in store for them. The kings of Connaught, Limerick, and Cork, who had meditated
tendering their fealty to John, now naturally held
aloof, and soon the faithful natives were driven by
the insults and injuries suffered at the hands of the
invaders into active revolt. Meanwhile the newcomers had completely alienated the early settlers,
depriving them of their hard-won conquests and dis-
tributing offices of importance and honour with a
complete disregard for the fitness of the candidates.
The Norman courtiers, used to the luxurious life of
large towns and the aristocratic campaigning of the
Continent, utterly refused to endure the hardships
inseparable from service in the interior of the country,
and clung to the seaboard towns where alone wine
was available. Hugh de Lacy and the barons who
had won and held Leinster by their strength and
military ability kept grimly aloof and watched

disaster after disaster overtake the incompetent and
inexperienced army of invasion.

Matters soon reached such a pitch that it was
clear that some man of ability must be put in command, and accordingly in the autumn of 1185 John
de Courcy, whose conquest of Ulster had proved him
to be a warrior of consummate skill and daring,
was appointed chief governor with excellent effect,
and two months later Prince John returned to
England. He had no difficulty in persuading his
infatuated father that his failure was due to the
treachery of Hugh de Lacy, and it was with un-
concealed delight that Henry heard of Lacy's murder
in 1186. Early in that same year Pope Urban III.
had acceded to Henry's request for the coronation of
John as king of Ireland, and had even sent him a
crown of gold and peacocks' feathers—borrowed
plumes sufficiently suitable for the empty head they
were to adorn. John was therefore despatched to
Ireland to seize Lacy's great fief into the king's
hand in August, but before he could sail news arrived
of the death of his brother Geoffrey, and he was recalled. For the remaining three years of his reign
Henry was too busy with English and foreign affairs
to devote his attention to Ireland.

CHAPTER VII

THE REBELLION OF THE YOUNG KING

HENRY had left Ireland, as we have seen, on 17th April 1172, and about the second week in May he crossed from Portsmouth to Barfleur with a considerable following, at least twenty-five ships accompanying him. On 17th May he met the cardinals at Savigny, and was informed by them of the terms offered by the pope for his reconciliation to the Church   It would seem that these included the entire abrogation of the Constitutions of Clarendon, and to this Henry absolutely declined to consent, declaring that sooner than accept these conditions he would return to Ireland. The diplomatic Bishop Arnulf of Lisieux now intervened and succeeded in effecting a compromise, and on Sunday, 21st May, Henry came to the cathedral of Avranches and was absolved from the guilt of the murder of Becket on a promise to comply with the modified requirements of the legates. He was to find the money to support two hundred men-at-arms for one year in the Holy Land, to go for three years on Crusade, to restore the property of the church of Canterbury, and take back into favour all who had suffered for their support of the archbishop ; he was also to support the claims of Alexander and his successors against the schismatics, to permit appeals to the pope in ecclesiastical causes, and to abolish all customs injurious to the Church which had been newly introduced in his reign. The wording of the last clause left matters exactly as they were at the beginning of the quarrel with Becket, for the whole point of the dispute was Henry's contention that the Constitutions were in force in the time of his grandfather. The final issue of the conflict was thus decidedly in Henry's favour, and the murder, instead of proving, as it must have done in the case of a less able man, disastrous, had actually been beneficial. The king's strength is also shown in his dealings with the four knights who had murdered the archbishop ; a weaker man would almost certainly have sacrificed the murderers to appease public opinion, but Henry, admitting that they had acted on his behalf though not in accord with his intentions, took no action against them, possibly not sorry to let ecclesiastical claims reduce themselves to a logical absurdity by showing that the Church could only deal with the ecclesiastical offence of the murder of an archbishop by the ineffective method of excommunication.

The young King Henry was present at the ceremony at Avranches and joined with his father in swearing to obey the terms imposed, so far as they were not personal to the elder king; but it would seem that the representatives of France and other important personages were absent, and it was therefore

arranged that the ceremony should be repeated at
a later date at Caen. The absolution was duly
repeated about Michaelmas, but whether at Caen
or again at Avranches is not quite clear. Meanwhile
Henry had arranged for the deferred coronation of
his son's wife Margaret, the daughter of King Louis.
It has already been mentioned that, much to her
father's anger, she had not been crowned with her
husband, but it would seem that Henry had had the
genuine intention of allowing her to be crowned
subsequently. He appears to have promised Becket
that he should officiate, and it may have been for this
purpose that Margaret crossed over to England in
September 1170. She remained at Winchester until
3rd April 1171, when she crossed again to Normandy,
and was no doubt with her husband at Christmas
that year, when the young Henry held his court at
Bur-le-Roi, to which flocked the chivalry in such
numbers that it is recorded that in one hall there
dined together a hundred and three knights whose
Christian name was William. In August 1172
Margaret and her husband went back to England,
and on the 27th of that month they were crowned
together in Winchester Cathedral by Rotrou, Archbishop of Rouen, and the Bishops of Evreux and
Worcester. Their stay was not of long duration, as
early in November thay were summoned back to
Normandy by the old king. They obeyed unwillingly,
but instead of joining the English court paid a visit
to King Louis, who seized the opportunity to urge

upon the young Henry that he should demand from
his father the complete sovereignty of either England
or Normandy, or at any rate something more substantial than the shadowy royalty which he had
hitherto enjoyed. The counsel fell on willing ears ;
the prince had long smarted under his father's strict
control and the surveillance of ministers who were
practically his masters, and he was in no mind to
remain a king without a kingdom and without even
a sufficient income.

After Christmas, which the young king and his
queen kept at Bonneville while the elder Henry and
Eleanor were at Chinon, the two Henrys went to
Montferrand and afterwards to Limoges to negotiate
for the marriage of John, now six years old, with
Alais, daughter and heir of the powerful Count
Hubert of Maurienne, lord of Savoy. The count
undertook to make a most liberal provision for the
young couple, but when it came to Henry's turn to
fix what he would bestow upon them he named the
castellanies of Chinon, Loudun, and Mirabeau. The
young Henry at once indignantly protested that these
castles belonged to him as Count of Anjou, and absolutely declined to make them over to his brother.
This, combined with his father's action in refusing to
increase either his power or his allowance and in
removing from his company certain young men of
bad influence, roused the young king's resentment,
which was sedulously fanned by his mother, Queen
Eleanor. The latter, egged on by her uncle, Ralph

de Faye, urged her son to open rebellion, and afterwards persuaded his brothers, Richard and Geoffrey, to join him in opposition to their father. At last, on 5th March, the young king slipped away, and evading pursuit reached the court of Louis.

The rebellion thus begun bore a formidable aspect and seemed to have every prospect of success. Young Henry was an admirable centre for the concentration of the disaffected. Tall, remarkably handsome, and adding to his father's charm of manner an open-handed liberality which the elder Henry lacked, he was already earning the reputation which he established a few years later as the flower of chivalry, while his apparently complete lack of solid qualities in no way detracted from his popularity. In the struggle with his father he could of course count upon the assistance of King Louis, and though that king was singularly incompetent his resources were very considerable. The more lawless English lords, whose wings had been clipped by Henry's anti-feudal legislation, might also be counted upon ; and in this category were old Hugh Bigot, Earl of Norfolk, the other Earl Hugh, he of Chester, the young Earl of Leicester, son of the loyal justiciar who had died in 1168, Earl Ferrers of Derby, and Roger Mowbray. The discontented lords whose lands lay within Henry's continental domains were still more numerous, and included the Counts of Ponthieu, Evreux, Eu, and Meulan, William de Tancarville, chamberlain of Normandy, and Geoffrey and Guy de Lusignan.

Amongst those who seem to have supported the young king out of affection for him rather than out of hatred of his father were William Marshal, younger son of Becket's adversary and one of the most brilliant knights of his time, Hasculf de Saint Hilaire, Robert Tregoz, and William de Dives. Further important allies were secured by recklessly liberal promises of reward : to Count Philip of Flanders young Henry promised the county of Kent with the castles of Dover and Rochester and £1000 of rent; to his brother, the Count of Boulogne, the county of Mortain and other lands ; to Theobald, Count of Blois, the castle of Amboise and £500 of rents from Anjou; and a little later, when the unsatisfactory state of affairs in Normandy rendered desirable a diversion in England, Westmoreland with Carlisle and possibly also Northumberland were offered to King William of Scotland, while to his brother David the earldom of Huntingdon and Cambridge was granted.

On the other hand, though his continental domains were seething with discontent, King Henry could count upon powerful support from the English magnates. The Earls of Cornwall, Surrey, Arundel, Essex, Northampton, and Salisbury could be relied upon ; Richard " Strongbow " of Pembroke was loyal, though too much engaged with affairs in Ireland to be of much assistance; and William of Gloucester, though married to the young Earl of Leicester's sister, would be at worst neutral. The best part of the baronage, headed by the great justiciar, Richard

de Luci, " the Loyal," were to be depended upon, and
included men of the military ability of Humphrey
de Bohun, Robert de Stuteville, William de Vesci,
and Odinell de Umfraville. The kings of Wales, David
ap Owain and the redoubtable Rhys ap Gruffudd,
with their hardy warriors, were also allies not to be
despised. The valuable support of the Church was
also, contrary to what might have been expected,
strongly on the elder king's side, the only conspicuous
exceptions being the Bishop of Durham and, curiously
enough, Henry's former ardent partisan, Arnulf of
Lisieux. To further strengthen his position Henry
now filled up the six vacant English bishoprics,
taking the opportunity to promote his faithful
archdeacons; Richard of Ilchester, Archdeacon of
Poictiers, receiving the see of Winchester, Geoffrey
Ridel of Canterbury that of Ely, and Reynold,
Archdeacon of Salisbury, that of Bath; Robert
Foliot, Archdeacon of Lincoln and brother of the
Bishop of London, obtained Hereford, Joscelin was
promoted from the deanery to the bishopric of
Chichester, and the great see of Lincoln was bestowed
upon the king's illegitimate son Geoffrey. In this
manner Henry showed his obedience to the papal
demand that the vacant sees should be filled, and at
the same time he obtained practical control of the
episcopal bench. The primacy was for a time left
unfilled, owing to disputes between the monks of
Canterbury and the bishops of the province, and to
other causes; but in June, Richard, Prior of Dover,

was elected by general consent, and, by a happy coincidence, on the day of his election there arrived a letter from the pope announcing that the martyred Thomas of Canterbury had been enrolled amongst the saints.

Thanks to his wise policy in encouraging the trading and mercantile communities and in protecting the small men from the oppression of the great, Henry had on his side the bulk of the populace and especially the citizens of London, Rouen, and the other great towns. Finally, he had great financial resources, and it was this abundance of money that turned the scale in his favour by enabling him not only to hire large numbers of mercenaries but also to buy off many of the French nobles who were supposed to be supporting his rebellious sons.

As soon as it was clear that his son had fled to raise the standard of rebellion Henry proceeded to Gisors and set that and his other frontier castles in a state of defence. While he was so doing a rumour reached the rebels that he was advancing to attack them and they at once prepared for battle. The young king had not yet been knighted, his father having intended that King Louis should bestow the dignity upon him; but feeling that it would befit his position as leader of the army he now hastily sought the honour of knighthood at the hands of his faithful comrade and instructor in the art of arms, William Marshal. The alarm proved false; Henry, so far from attacking, retired to Rouen,

I

where he spent the greater part of the next four months hunting and apparently ignoring the outbreak, but really keeping a watchful eye upon events and waiting the opportunity to strike a crushing blow.

About the last week in June Henry appears to have made a hurried visit to England, going straight to Northampton, spending four days there, and then returning at once to Rouen.[1] Affairs in England were calculated to give rise to some anxiety. Although so many castles had been thrown down or taken into the king's hand since the beginning of his reign a considerable number still remained in private hands, and of these at least a score were now held for the rebels. On the east coast Hugh Bigot held Framlingham and Bungay; in the Midlands, Huntingdon was held for David of Scotland; the Earl of Leicester had Leicester, Mountsorel, and Groby; the Earl Ferrers Tutbury and Duffield; while Chester was held for Earl Hugh. In the north the Bishop of Durham had fortified Durham, Norham, and Northallerton, and Mowbray held Thirsk, Malzeard, and Axholme; Hamo de Masci had castles at Dunham and Ullerwood, Geoffrey de Costantin at Stockport, and Richard de Morville at Lauder, and there were a number of smaller fortresses which might prove

---

[1] The Pipe Roll, 19 Henry II., shows an expenditure of £32, 6s. 5d. for the king's maintenance at Northampton for four days; and it would seem that he travelled without luggage, as over £72 was spent at the same time on the outfit which the sheriff provided for the king. None of the chroniclers notice this flying visit, but the evidence appears to favour the end of June as the most probable date.

centres of danger. The castles in the hands of the king and his supporters must have been at least five times as numerous, and the royal officers speedily set in order those in the districts most likely to be affected—the south-east, exposed to the raids of Flemish and French, and the north, where the Scots were to be feared. Porchester, Southampton, and Winchester were strengthened, so were Arundel, Chichester, and Hastings ; in Kent much money was spent on the castles of Dover, Canterbury, Rochester, and Chilham ; the Tower of London was of course a centre of activity ; at Oreford the outer defences were strengthened ; Walton, Colchester, and Norwich were garrisoned ; so were Hertford, Cambridge, Wisbeach, and Lincoln. Windsor, Oxford, Berkhamstead, Wallingford, Kenilworth, Warwick, Worcester, Nottingham, and the Peak carried the chain of royal strongholds across the country, while in the north were York, Bowes, Richmond, Carlisle, Prudhoe, Appleby, Wark, and Newcastle. For the present the chief centre of danger seemed to be Leicester, and it was no doubt as a result of the king's flying visit to Northampton that operations were set on foot early in July against Leicester.

About the time that Henry returned to Rouen, on 29th June, Count Philip of Flanders captured Aumâle, probably by the connivance of its defender, Count William of Aumâle, and, after a more energetic resistance, the castle of Driencourt. This last success, however, was neutralised by the death of

Philip's brother, Count Matthew of Boulogne. Meanwhile the French army under King Louis and the young King Henry was vainly besieging Verneuil. Hugh de Lacy and Hugh de Beauchamp, who were in command of the defence, had no difficulty in repelling their attacks, but after a month's siege provisions ran short in the outermost of the three " bourgs " into which the town was divided, and the inhabitants agreed that if they were not relieved before 9th August they would surrender, the French on their side swearing to do them no harm. Henry, realising that instant action was necessary, advanced at once, burning the Earl of Leicester's abandoned castle of Breteuil on the way. When the two armies were in sight of one another on 8th August Louis sent envoys and obtained a truce until the next day, and Henry, not suspecting his good faith, retired to Conches. Next day Louis demanded the surrender of the bourg in accordance with the former agreement, and at once treacherously set it on fire and, adding cowardice to treachery, fled back to France, hotly pursued with great slaughter by Henry. The centre of action now shifted to Brittany, where the turbulent Breton nobles had risen under Ralph of Fougères and the Earl of Chester. Against them Henry sent a strong force of Brabantine mercenaries under William de Humez, who inflicted a very severe defeat on the rebels, capturing Hasculf de Saint Hilaire, William Patric and others, and driving the remainder of the force into the castle of Dol. A messenger was sent off at full gallop to Henry at Rouen, and by an almost incredibly rapid forced march he covered the whole distance from Rouen to Dol, over 150 miles, in two days.[1] Earl Hugh and Ralph of Fougères, seeing that resistance was hopeless, surrendered on 29th August, and by this single stroke eighty persons of rank and position and a number of men of lesser estate were captured and the rebellion in Brittany stamped out. The time now seemed ripe for a reconciliation, and on 25th September Henry met his three sons and King Louis near Gisors. The terms offered by the king to his sons were liberal in the extreme, but the French king had no wish to see peace restored and he persuaded them to reject the terms. The Earl of Leicester also, who had all arrangements made for an invasion of England, did his insolent best to keep the quarrel alive.

We have seen that early in July preparations had been made for the siege of Leicester. On the 22nd of that month the town surrendered to the Earl of Cornwall and Richard de Luci; the inhabitants were allowed to withdraw to St. Albans and other places of refuge and the town was set on fire. The castle, however, still held out, and in September news from the north caused the siege to be raised. King William of Scotland, having vainly offered his services to the elder Henry in return for a grant of Northum-

---

[1] All the authorities agree as to the rapidity of Henry's dash to Dol. Presumably he had with him only a small mounted escort.

berland, accepted the younger Henry's promise of
Westmoreland and assembled a large army to reduce
the northern counties. His first move was against
the castle of Wark, where Roger de Stuteville was in
command ; Roger obtained a truce of forty days
and the Scottish army passed on, ravaging and burning as they went, and after an ineffectual attack
on William de Vesci's castle of Alnwick captured
Warkworth Castle. Newcastle, held for the king by
Roger Fitz-Richard, Lord of Warkworth, proved too
strong for the invaders, and their efforts were next
directed against Carlisle. Here Robert de Vaux
made a gallant defence, and news arriving of the
advance of the English relieving force the Scots re-
treated to Roxburgh in full flight. Richard de Luci,
with the troops he had brought from Leicester, and
Humphrey de Bohun, with a detachment of mercenary
cavalry, pursued them across the border and burnt
Berwick. But news reached them that the Earl of
Leicester had landed with a force of Flemings at
Walton on 29th September. Bohun at once turned
southwards, while Luci negotiated with the Scottish
king before the news of Leicester's landing could
reach the latter. A truce was obtained to last until
January, and by the Bishop of Durham's mediation
this was afterwards extended to April 1174.

The Earl of Leicester, on landing, had spent four
days in a fruitless endeavour to capture Walton
Castle, but finding it too strong to be taken, although
Earl Hugh of Norfolk had brought a siege train

to his assistance, he turned aside and attacked Haughley. This fortress, held by Ranulph de Broc, Becket's old adversary, was speedily captured and given to the flames, and then the earl's initiative appears to have died out and he was content to quarter himself idly at Framlingham until Earl Hugh gave him a strong hint that he was outstaying his welcome. At last he decided to try and reach Leicester, and on 17th October he started, with the intention of passing to the north of Bury St. Edmunds. At the latter town the royalists, under Humphrey de Bohun, had been reinforced by troops under the Earls of Cornwall and Arundel, local levies under Roger le Bigod, the loyal son of old Earl Hugh, and Hugh de Cressi, and a detachment of hardy fighting men from Ireland. Setting out with St. Edmund's banner at their head they came upon the Flemings at Fornham-St. Geneveve. In actual numbers the advantage lay with the Earl of Leicester, but his followers were almost entirely infantry of poor quality, quite unfitted to cope with the powerful cavalry opposed to them, and it was only a matter of minutes before the Flemings had been ridden down and scattered, a prey for the country people, who bore them no good-will. Earl Robert and his cousin, Hugh de Chastel, were captured, and the gallant Countess Peronelle, clad in mail, falling into a stream in her flight, was with difficulty rescued from a death which she preferred to the disgrace of surrender. A halt was now made and forces collected to crush Earl Hugh, but with the aid of his wealth he bought a truce for himself and permission for the Flemish mercenaries still in England to leave the country unharmed.

Henry, having seen the captured earl and countess safely lodged in the castle of Falaise, led an army into Anjou in November and captured Preuilly, La Haye, and Champigny with a large number of men of rank. The year 1173 thus ended favourably for the elder king, and truces with the kings of France and Scotland ensured peace until the close of Easter, 31st March 1174. But with the beginning of April the struggle began again. The Scottish king crossed the border and besieged Wark, raiding as far as Bamborough, where William de Vesci's castle proved too strong to be attacked. Roger de Stuteville offered a vigorous defence, and the besiegers' artillery proving more deadly to themselves than to the garrison, King William abandoned the siege of Wark and concentrated his efforts on Carlisle. He had been joined by Roger Mowbray and Adam de Port, a Norman baron who had been banished and deprived of his English estates in 1172 for conspiring against Henry, and his army included the inevitable execrated Flemish mercenaries. Ruthless as these Flemish adventurers were, they were less inhuman than the savage Highlanders and men of Galloway who accompanied them. From Carlisle plundering bands ravaged and destroyed the northern counties, while more warlike expeditions captured the border forts of Liddel and Harbottle. Far more serious was the tame surrender of Appleby Castle: the aged Gospatric, son of Orm, the English constable of the castle, was possibly too old for his responsible position, and his lack of confidence would seem to have affected the garrison, amongst whom were the steward of Hugh de Morville, the murderer of Becket, and one John de Morville, probably connections of Richard de Morville, who was a prominent supporter of the Scottish king. This success was followed up by the capture, after a desperate resistance, of Brough-under-Stanemore, and the general trend of affairs induced Robert de Vaux to obtain a truce for Carlisle on undertaking to surrender at Michaelmas if not relieved before that date.

Henry, after assuring himself of the loyalty of Maine and Anjou in the spring of 1174, had entered Poitou and inflicted a crushing defeat on the troops of his son Richard at Saintes in May. Messages had been reaching him for some time past from the justiciar, who was besieging Huntingdon, urging his return to England, and on his arrival at Bonneville in Normandy on 24th June he was met by Richard of Ilchester, bishop-elect of Winchester, with news of the gravity of affairs. There was no mistaking the significance of the selection of Richard—" they could not have sent a more urgent messenger, unless they had sent the Tower of London "—and Henry at once prepared to cross to England. He accordingly embarked at Barfleur on 7th July, and being determined to leave no centres of disaffection behind him, he carried with him the Earls of Chester and Leicester, Queen Eleanor, who had been captured the previous year trying to reach the French court in male disguise, and Queen Margaret. The weather was stormy but the wind was in the right direction, and Henry bade the shipmen set sail, saying solemnly, " If what I purpose is for the peace of Church and people, and if the King of Heaven has decreed that peace shall be restored by my coming, then in His mercy may He grant me a safe passage. But if He has turned His face from me and has decreed to afflict the kingdom with a rod, then may it never be mine to set foot on shore." The voyage to Southampton was accomplished in safety, and Henry at once proceeded, fasting and with all signs of humility, to Canterbury, where on 12th July he performed public penance at the tomb of St. Thomas. The Bishop of London delivered an address on the king's behalf, disavowing all share in the murder, but admitting that his rash words had been the actual cause of it ; then, after long remaining in prayer at the tomb, the king submitted to a ceremonial scourging at the hands of all the monks of the convent of Christ Church. Finally he made a grant of lands to the monastery in memory of the martyr, and probably at the same time settled a small income upon Becket's married sister, Roese,[1] his

---

[1] The Pipe Roll of 21 Henry II. shows a pension of 33s. 4d. paid to her for the last quarter of the twentieth year. She seems to have died in 1188, as the pension was then paid to her son John.

other sister, Mary, having been appointed in the previous year Abbess of Berking.

The news of Henry's landing put an end to the plans of the younger king for an invasion of England, which he had contemplated in company with Philip of Flanders. He had even gone so far as to send over three hundred picked Flemish knights under Ralph de la Haye in June. They had landed at Orewell, placed themselves under the command of Earl Hugh of Norfolk, and, after being repulsed from Dunwich, had captured the wealthy city of Norwich by treachery and gained thereby great plunder if little military advantage. This occurred on 18th June, and the news apparently caused the justiciar to relinquish the siege of Huntingdon, leaving Earl Simon of Northampton, who claimed the earldom of Huntingdon, to win the castle and the county for himself. As we have already seen an urgent message was despatched to the king, and about the same time Robert de Vaux obtained conditions for Carlisle. The Scottish army being thus set free for fresh enterprises Roger Mowbray urged King William to move southwards to his assistance, his strongholds of Axholme and Malzeard having fallen before the troops of Geoffrey, the king's illegitimate son, the young bishop-elect of Lincoln, and Thirsk being threatened. William preferred the less hazardous course of keeping near his own borders, and laid siege to Odinal de Umfraville's castle of Prudhoe. The castle was strong and well provisioned, and

Odinal succeeded in getting away to raise forces for
its relief. Preparing to retreat into his own country,
the Scottish king sent detachments of his army
under Earl Duncan, the Earl of Angus, and Richard
de Morville to ravage the country, while he with a
small body of knights made a demonstration against
Alnwick. The English forces under Ranulf de
Glanvill, Odinal de Umfraville, Robert de Stuteville,
William de Vesci, and Bernard de Baillol left Newcastle
at daybreak on 13th July, and, favoured by a mist,
surprised King William and his attendants close
to Alnwick. William the Lion did not surrender
tamely, but, mounting his horse, led his men against
the foe. The odds were too heavy, however; the
king's charger was killed and he himself pinned
to the ground by its fall, Roger de Mowbray and
Adam de Port fled for safety, but the Scottish
knights fought for their lord so long as resistance
was possible. Thus on the day, possibly even at the
hour, on which Henry completed his penance at the
tomb of St. Thomas his most dangerous opponent
was made prisoner. The good news was despatched
at once by a mounted messenger, who found Henry
resting at London, where he had had a most en-
thusiastic reception upon his arrival. The king,
who was unwell, was asleep, but the messenger
would brook no delay, and the news of William's
capture, which Henry could at first hardly believe,
proved good medicine for the sick man. The nobles
at court were at once told the news, and next day

SEAL OF WILLIAM THE LION (†)

all the bells of London's six score churches rang in joy that the rebellion in England was at an end.

A few days later the king advanced to Huntingdon, which surrendered to him on 21st July. He then turned to attack Earl Hugh's castle of Framlingham, and by the 24th had advanced with his siege train as far as Seleham; but next day the earl met him there, gave up his castles of Bungay and Framlingham, and agreed to pay a heavy fine for his offence and to make amends for the damage wrought by his soldiers; he was at once restored to his earldom, and his Flemish troops were permitted to leave the country unmolested, but not to take any property with them. During this interview, which took place on horseback in the open air, the king was kicked on the leg by the horse of Tostes de St. Omer, a Templar of prominence, but the injury did not prevent his going on to Northampton, where the last act of the rebellion in England was played. Bishop Hugh Puiset, who had brought over a detachment of Flemings under command of his nephew, the Count of Bar, on the very day on which the Scottish king was captured, had sent back the infantry at once, but had retained his nephew and his men-at-arms until the fortune of war had set definitely in Henry's favour; he now made submission, gave up his castles of Durham, Northallerton, and Norham, and dismissed his foreign allies. The Earl of Clare, who was believed to have been plotting action with Gilbert Munfichet when the latter fortified his London

castle, tendered assurances of loyalty. Roger Mowbray surrendered Thirsk; Ansketil Malory, who had
defended Leicester so well, and had even attacked
and defeated the loyalists at Northampton, gave up
his master's castles of Leicester, Groby, and Mountsorel; and Earl Ferrers, who not long before had
sacked Nottingham, gave up Tutbury, which had
been besieged for some time past by Rhys and his
Welshmen. Rhys was rewarded by a grant of the
castle and district of " Emelin," while the loyalty
of David ap Owain of North Wales was recompensed
by the hand of Emma, King Henry's half-sister.

Although affairs in England had been settled so
satisfactorily there was no time to be lost; taking
advantage of Henry's absence King Louis had
pressed forward with the young King Henry and invested Rouen. The town was devoted to the elder
Henry's interests; it was well provisioned and was
in no great danger, but it was clearly desirable that
it should be relieved as soon as possible, and on 8th
August Henry sailed for Barfleur, carrying his more
important prisoners with him and taking back not
only the Brabantine mercenaries he had brought
over in June but also a number of Welsh troops.
These latter on 12th August, the day after their
arrival at Rouen, crossed the Seine and made a
bold and successful raid on the French camp, and
next day a sally from the town resulted in the easy
destruction of the defensive works of the besiegers'
camp. When the war had opened just a year before,

in August 1173, with the siege of Verneuil, Louis
had shown a blend of treachery, cowardice, and incompetence, and now that the war was closing with
this siege of Rouen his conduct displayed the same
features. Just before Henry's arrival, on St. Laurence's Day (10th August), the French king had
declared a truce in honour of the saint and then
made secret preparations for storming the city;
fortunately some priests, who happened to be on
the belfry looking at the view, saw the movement
in the enemy's camp and rang the tocsin; the citizens
flew to arms, and the French took therefrom no advantage but dishonour and disgrace. On the day
after the successful sally the French burnt their
siege engines and fled, Louis staving off pursuit by
proposing a conference at Malannai next day, but
again breaking his word and flying into France.

Negotiations were opened on 8th September at
Gisors, but as Richard was still defying his father in
Poitou a settlement was postponed and Henry went
in pursuit of his warlike son. A couple of weeks
sufficed to bring Richard to terms, and on the last
day of September conditions of peace were drawn
up. The followers of the young king were released
from the allegiance they had sworn to him, and were
received back into the king's favour and as full
possession of their lands as they had at the time
war broke out; prisoners were released without
ransom, except such as had already come to terms
and also excepting the King of Scotland, the Earls

of Leicester and Chester, and Ralph of Fougères ;
all castles that had been built or strengthened during
the rebellion were to be restored to their former
condition, and, indeed, so far as possible everything
was to resume its previous existence. The young
King Henry was granted two castles in Normandy
and a yearly allowance of £15,000 Angevin money
(£3600 English) ; Richard should have two castles
of no strategic importance in Poitou and half the
revenues of that province, and Geoffrey half the inheritance of Constance, daughter of Count Conan
of Brittany, and the whole when he married her.
At the same time the young king agreed to the
bestowal upon his youngest brother, John, of the
castles of Nottingham and Marlborough, and £1000
from the English revenues, as well as castles and
rents in Normandy, Anjou, and Maine. Richard
and Geoffrey then did homage to their father, but
this ceremony was dispensed with in Henry's case
out of deference to his rank of king.   Finally, in
December, King William the Lion obtained his re-
lease from the prison at Falaise by becoming the
vassal of Henry and undertaking to hold Scotland
under the English king.   To ensure the fulfilment of
this treaty the castles of Edinburgh, Roxburgh,
Berwick, Jedburgh, and Stirling were surrendered to
Henry.   The close of 1174 thus found Henry completely triumphant and the formidable combination
of his enemies absolutely shattered.

SEALS OF GEOFFREY, SON OF HENRY II, AND CONSTANCE OF BRITTANY, HIS WIFE (†)

CHAPTER VIII

HENRY AND HIS SONS—HIS DOWNFALL AND DEATH

THE economic effects of the rebellion were far-reaching. Those who had been involved in it returned, it is true, nominally to the position in which they had been before the outbreak, but their lands had been systematically ravaged, their castles given to the flames, and blackened ruins told for a generation the tale of their disastrous failure. So far as England was concerned these effects were more localised and less extensive. During the war Mowbray's castles of Kirkby Malzeard and Axholme had been destroyed, and at its close the same fate befell Thirsk. Thetford and Brackley and the two Kentish castles of Allington and Saltwood had been dismantled before the end of 1174, and so had Geoffrey de Turville's castle of Weston. Next year saw the overthrow of Groby and Tutbury ; Dudley, the castle of Earl Ferrers' son-in-law, Gervase Painel, was razed and its owner fined 500 marks for his share in the revolt, his neighbour and comrade in arms, Hamo de Masci, being at the same time fined 300 marks. The strongholds of Huntingdon and Leicester were rendered incapable of again

resisting the king's forces, and the great English
military architect and engineer, Ælnoth, came down
to supervise the levelling of the walls of Framlingham Castle and the filling of its fosse. For strategic
reasons the fort at Walton, which had successfully
resisted the Flemish invaders, was destroyed in
1176, and also the keep of Bennington, and the
Bishop of Durham only saved his castle of Northallerton by a payment of 2000 marks. What other
castles disappeared we do not know, but such as
remained were taken into the king's hands, the
Earl of Gloucester yielding Bristol and Gloucester
with great reluctance.

The expenses of the war must have strained
Henry's finances severely. For the expeditions on
the Scottish border alone we know that Ranulph
de Glanville and Robert de Stuteville paid over
£2000 to their troops, and the cost of the mercenaries
employed on the Continent must have been very
heavy. A large but quite uncertain sum must have
been obtained from the ransom of the many important prisoners taken, and further contributions
were levied in the form of fines. The Earl of
Leicester was impleaded by Bertram de Verdon,
Sheriff of Leicestershire, for injuries done by his men
and fined 500 marks. Nine citizens of York who had
sided with the rebels were fined 1300 marks between
them, several of them being also fined smaller sums
for receiving goods belonging to Flemings. These
latter had been banished from England, saving their

lives at the expense of their property, and the township of Selby was fined £5 for allowing Flemings to
carry away their goods, William of Selby 5 marks
for not detaining Flemings whom he saw pass through
the town, and Fulk of Selby £10 for hiring his ship
to the Flemings. For the most part these foreigners
were clothworkers, and their forfeited property,
consisting chiefly of wool, did not yield any great
sum. A more fruitful source of income arose from
the estates of the Earl of Leicester and his companions during the time that they were in arms
against the king, and from these only about £300
were obtained between September 1174 and the
restoration of the estates to their owners Apart
from the 2600 marks assessed upon the citizens of
York, the Earl of Leicester, Gervase Painel, and
Hamo de Masci, £500 was raised by smaller fines
upon persons who had sold horses or armour or
given other assistance to the rebels. Even adding in
Earl Hugh's fine of 700 marks and the 500 marks
which Gospatric was fined for the surrender of
Appleby, the total amount accounted for at the
exchequer as wrung from the vanquished party
seems to have fallen far short of £4000. Searching
for some device to fill his empty coffers Henry hit
upon the idea of vigorously punishing all offences
against the Forest Laws which had been committed
during the time of the disturbances. Accordingly,
in August 1175, he held pleas of the forest at Nottingham and afterwards at York in person and sent

special commissioners to hold similar pleas in other
counties. The baronage protested, and Richard de
Luci produced the king's own writ issued at the
time of the war, apparently suspending the Forest
Laws and authorising any person to take wood and
venison in the royal forests. It is as difficult to
understand why Henry issued such a writ as it is
to see upon what grounds he set it aside. Possibly
a writ intended to apply to certain special cases,
such as the taking of venison for the provisioning
of the royal troops or of timber for military works,
had by a misunderstanding or error of wording
been made to apply generally, and Henry declined
to accept responsibility for the mistake. However
this may be, it is clear that his action in pressing
these pleas was at least a piece of sharp practice,
and the heavy fines exacted can hardly be regarded
in the circumstances as anything but extortion.
The sum of the fines inflicted appears to have been
£13,450, and although much of this was not paid
at once and some was in the end remitted, the
eventual yield seems to have been quite £10,000.
About 1700 persons were amerced; and when it is
remembered that to these must be added a large
number of cases in which whole townships were
fined, it is clear that the total number of persons
affected must have been very large. A few fortunate
counties, such as Kent, Sussex, Norfolk, and Suffolk,
contained no royal forests, but elsewhere every class
of man was swept into the legal net, from the great

baron to the villein and including the clergy. Henry had indeed succeeded in wringing from the papal legate, Cardinal Ugoccione, the concession that the clergy should be subject to the Forest Laws.

The legate had been sent over to settle the rival claims of the sees of Canterbury and York, but his arrival only tended to aggravate matters. At a synod held at Westminster on 18th March 1176, the endeavours of Archbishop Roger of York to oust Richard of Canterbury from his seat of honour on the legate's right hand led to a disgraceful scuffle, in which Archbishop Roger was attacked by the supporters of the southern primate, knocked down, and in the end ignominiously ejected from the chapel. The legate indignantly dismissed the synod and was with difficulty persuaded to retain his official position. In July he left England, having accomplished practically nothing in the matter of the rival sees. If popular rumour was correct in believing that he had been sounded by Henry on the question of a divorce from Queen Eleanor, in this matter also there had been no result. The one important result of his visit had been that the clergy were for the future to be subject to the Forest Laws and also to plead in the king's court in matters touching lay fees. It is said that by way of compensation Henry recognised their exemption from lay jurisdiction in all other matters, agreed not to make a practice of retaining vacant bishoprics and abbeys in his hands, and granted that the murder of a clerk should be punished by forfeiture. Even if these concessions were made they were far from reconciling those of the clerical party who still held Becket's ideal of the supremacy of the Church.

Restored to favour with the pope and victorious over as formidable a combination of his enemies as could well be formed against him, Henry was now at the height of his power, recognised throughout Europe as a prince whose friendship was worth seeking. In his court at Westminster on 12th November 1176, might have been seen ambassadors from the Emperor Manuel of Constantinople, the Emperor Frederic, the Duke of Saxony, the Count of Flanders, and the Archbishop of Rheims. About the same time also came a joint mission from the Kings of Castile and Navarre asking Henry to arbitrate between them in a dispute about certain castles and other territory. Accordingly, in the following March Henry heard the arguments of the rival embassies and gave his decision after consultation with the peers of his court, sentencing each side to make restitution to the other and further condemning the King of Castile to pay to Navarre 3000 maravedis a year for the next ten years. This King Alphonso of Castile had married Henry's daughter Eleanor in 1170, and about the time that the subject of this arbitration was first broached, at the end of 1176, another of Henry's daughters, Joan, was on her way to marry King William of Sicily. Negotiations for the marriage had been opened earlier in the year, and after her

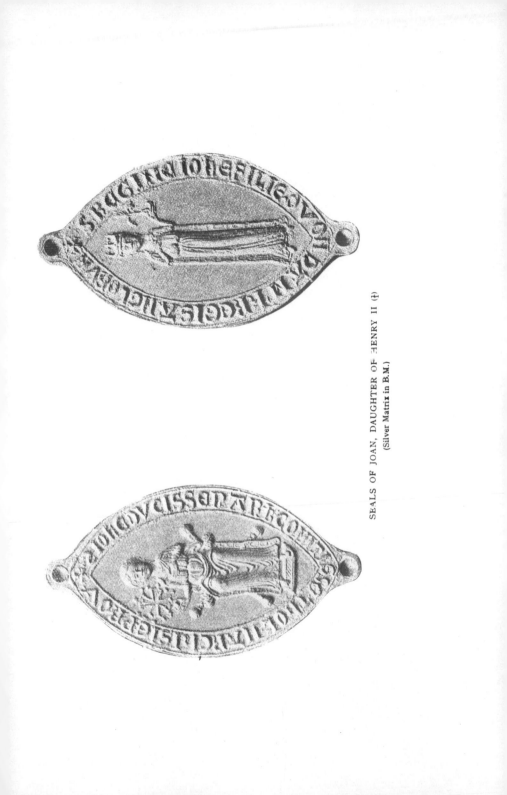

SEALS OF JOAN, DAUGHTER OF HENRY II (⅓)

(Silver Matrix in B.M.)

trousseaux had been bought in London, at a cost
of over £100 (say £2500 of modern money), she
travelled through France with a brilliant retinue to
St. Gilles, where she found awaiting her the Sicilian
nobles and the Bishop of Norwich. The unfortunate
bishop had been sent on ahead earlier in the year
to Sicily to make final arrangements and had had
a very rough time; the country through which he
passed was suffering from famine and he could hardly
get provisions for himself or his horse; accommodation sometimes failed completely, so that he had to
sleep on the rocks or sand of the seashore, and when
he had a roof over his head he found that the fleas
had no reverence for his episcopal or ambassadorial
dignity, so that he was very pleased to complete
his mission by handing the princess over to the
Sicilians and to hurry back to England in time for
the Christmas festivities at the court at Nottingham.

Two other marriages occupied the king's attention
about this time. The young daughter of Count
Hubert of Maurienne having died, Henry had to
find another heiress as bride for his favourite son
John, and ultimately decided that the great estates
of the Earl of Gloucester would make a suitable
endowment for the landless prince. The earl had
three daughters, of whom two were already married
to the Earl of Hertford and the Count of Evreux,
and Henry now prevailed upon the earl to agree that
all his estates should be settled upon the remaining
daughter, Isabel, and that she should be betrothed

to John, for whom the king had also reserved the great estates of his uncle, Earl Reynold of Cornwall, upon the latter's death in 1175, with similar disregard for the rights of his daughters and lawful heirs. Having settled this matter to his satisfaction Henry next found himself confronted with the question of Richard's matrimonial affairs. Richard had long been pledged to marry Alais, daughter of King Louis, and she had been, in accordance with the usual practice of the time, brought up at the court of her intended father-in-law. She was now about twenty and the King of France was pressing for the marriage to be performed, and in 1177 a papal legate was despatched from Rome with instructions to lay Henry's dominions under an interdict if he should refuse to carry out the agreement. In August of that year Henry crossed to Normandy and next month met the legate at Rouen, and on 21st September held a conference with King Louis at Ivry. At this conference the promise that Richard should marry Alais seems to have been renewed in an informal way, but Henry had no intention of fulfilling it, and indeed it seems probable that he was at this time himself the lover of the princess, who had succeeded the famous Rosamund Clifford in his affections when that beautiful favourite died.[1]

---

[1] " Fair Rosamund " was buried at Godstow Abbey, where the king set up a wonderfully carved monument to her memory. As we find fifty marks paid " for work at Godstow " in 1177, the first of a number of similar payments, it is probable that she had been buried there the previous year.

A more important effect of the conference at Ivry
was the treaty then drawn up between the two
kings, composing their differences and agreeing to
submit such points as still remained in dispute to
arbitration, and also agreeing to go together on
crusade to the Holy Land. Henry probably never
had the slightest intention of going to Jerusalem ;
indeed to have done so, leaving behind him such
disloyal and unprincipled young scoundrels as his
sons had proved themselves to be, would have been
madness, even if he had felt any particular interest
in the fate of the Holy Land. It will be remembered
that the terms upon which Henry was absolved from
the guilt of the murder of Becket had included the
payment of a large sum for the support of the
warriors in Palestine and his personal participation
in a crusade for three years. The first of these ob-
ligations he would seem to have discharged early in
1177, when the Earl of Essex and other English
knights went with Count Philip of Flanders to the
East, as William de Braose was sent "to carry the
king's alms to the Templars." The three years'
crusade was commuted for the foundation of three
monasteries, and Henry, whose partiality for monastic
establishments was by no means marked, contrived
to interpret this obligation in a way consistent with
the strictest economy. Finding that the secular
canons of Waltham had become remiss in the performance of their duties, he ejected them from their
collegiate church, with the connivance of their dean,

Guy Rufus, and replaced them by canons regular
of the Augustinian order. In the same way, finding
the lives of the nuns at Amesbury far from satisfactory, he turned them out, pensioning off the
abbess, and put in their place other nuns from the
Norman abbey of Fontevrault. Both of these trans-
formations took place in the latter half of 1177,
and for the next few years the work of rebuilding
and enlarging at Waltham and Amesbury were
carried on at the king's expense on a fairly generous
scale. The third monastery was a new foundation,
a small priory of Carthusians established at Witham
in Somerset. It would seem that Henry brought
over a few brethren from the famous monastery of
Chartreuse early in 1175, but gave them no assistance
and took no further steps towards establishing
them in permanent buildings. The first prior abandoned his post in despair and the next died soon
after his arrival at Witham ; Henry then succeeded
with much difficulty in persuading the Prior of
Chartreuse to send Hugh of Avalon, a monk of equal
ability and piety ; but when he came he had to
endure the same heartbreaking round of delays,
evasions, and unfulfilled promises, and it was not
until about 1180, when Henry discovered the true
worth and charm of his personality and became his
close friend, that the king made any endeavour to
complete the priory of Witham. It was characteristic of Henry that when the prior expressed
his wish for a copy of the Holy Scriptures for the

use of his brethren, the king compelled the monks of
Winchester to give up an elaborately written copy,
which they had just completed for their own use,
and presented it to the grateful monks of Witham.
It was equally characteristic of Hugh that, when he
learnt how the precious volume had been provided,
he insisted upon returning it to its rightful owners.

The warm affection which the king lavished upon
Hugh led many people to believe that the latter was
Henry's son, a belief strengthened by a certain
likeness observable between the two. And indeed
the likeness was not confined to physical traits, for
Hugh, with all his piety and austerity, was quick-
tempered and quick-witted and had as keen ap
preciation for a joke as had Henry himself, and
fully realised that a witty as well as a soft answer
may turn away wrath. On one occasion, having
incurred the king's wrath by excommunicating one
of his foresters, he was summoned to Woodstock
and found Henry and his courtiers sitting in a circle
on the grass. To intimate his displeasure the king
ignored Hugh's salutation and maintained a sulky
silence, the attendant nobles following his example ;
Hugh calmly pushed aside an earl and sat down
next to the king, who, incapable of resting idle,
called for a needle and thread and began to stitch
a torn leather finger-stall which he was wearing on
his left hand. Hugh watched him for a minute
and then said dryly, " How like you are now to your
cousins of Falaise ! " The impudence of the remark

appealed to Henry, who lay back and roared with laughter, and then himself explained to such of his courtiers as had not grasped the point that the allusion was to his descent, through William the Conqueror, from the peasant girl of Falaise, a town famous for its skinners and leatherworkers. This incident occurred after Hugh had been promoted, in 1186, from the priory of Witham to the bishopric of Lincoln, which had been held from 1173 to 1182 by the king's acknowledged bastard, Geoffrey, who, however, preferring rather to fleece than to tend his sheep, had never been consecrated to the see.

It is curious that Henry, himself careless of religion and actively antagonistic to the Church, should have lavished his warmest affection upon two men destined after their death to rank in the calendar of saints. The intimate friend of his early years became St. Thomas of Canterbury, and the chosen associate of the closing years of his reign was destined to become St. Hugh of Lincoln. The claims to saintship of the two men were singularly different; Thomas was one of those arrogant, fighting ecclesiastics who identify the cause of the Church with themselves and " take the kingdom of heaven by violence," while Hugh was a man of peace, one of those who identify themselves with the cause of God, to whom beatification comes as the natural reward for the blessings they have themselves bestowed upon their flocks. Of the two St. Thomas inevitably made the greater impression upon the

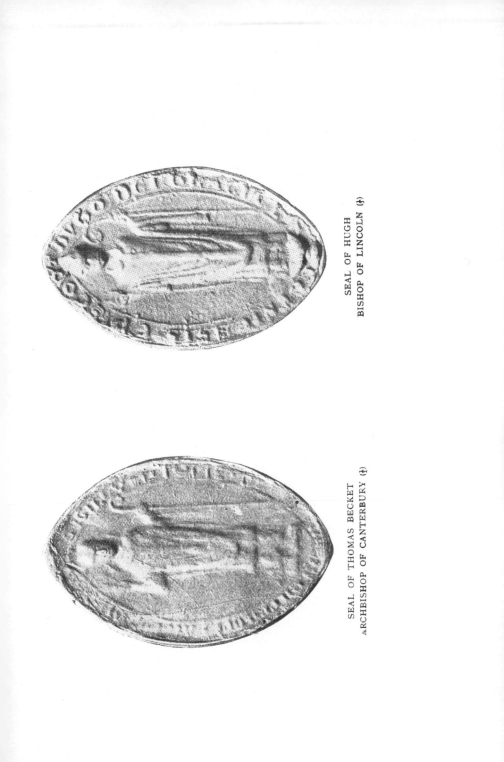

SEAL OF THOMAS BECKET
ARCHBISHOP OF CANTERBURY (†)

SEAL OF HUGH
BISHOP OF LINCOLN (†)

popular imagination, and his shrine was a centre of pilgrimage long before St. Hugh had even left his obscure priory for the great bishopric of Lincoln. A great impulse was no doubt given to the adoration of St. Thomas by the events of 1174, when the capture of the King of Scotland followed so immediately upon Henry's penance at Canterbury. In the twelfth century people did not talk of coincidence or propound elaborate theories that the concentration of Henry's mind upon the desire for victory had acted upon the brain centres of Ranulph de Glanville's subconsciousness and spurred him on to action. They simply accepted as a fact the personal intervention of St. Thomas, and Henry himself countenanced that view by going with his royal son on a pilgrimage of thanksgiving to Canterbury on 28th May 1175. Later in that year the young Queen Margaret visited the shrine " for the sake of prayer," and it is not improbable that we have the partial fulfilment of her petitions in the birth of a son at Paris in June 1177 ; but if so the answer to her prayers was only partial, for the child lived barely long enough to be christened William, and died within three days of his birth. A still more remarkable tribute to the fame of St. Thomas was paid in 1179. At that time King Louis was arranging for the coronation of his son Philip, then fourteen years old, but just before the date fixed for the ceremony the boy fell ill as the result of a hunting misadventure. Casting about in his mind for a suitable spiritual advocate it was not unnatural that the king's choice should fall upon Thomas of Canterbury ; if he had come so effectually to the help of his old adversary Henry he might surely be relied upon to assist his old supporter Louis. King Henry readily acceded to the French king's request for a safe conduct and met him in person at Dover on 22nd August, whence the two kings went next day to Canterbury. Here King Louis offered his petition at the tomb of the saint and enriched the convent with the grant of a yearly render of wine and exemption from customs for goods exported for their use from France.

On his return to France the king found his son convalescent, and in November the postponed coronation took place, the younger Henry being amongst those present. But before this date King Louis himself had been struck down with paralysis, and after nine months' illness he died on 18th September 1180. Death was busy about this time ; Richard de Luci, the great justiciar, had died in July 1179 at the priory of Lesnes, which he had founded ; Pope Alexander III. died in August 1181, and Roger, Archbishop of York, in the following November. In Louis, Henry lost an old antagonist, but one whose weakness and incompetence had been a source of strength to the English king. Henry had never pursued an aggressive policy towards France and had never attempted to crush Louis or even to throw off his nominal suzerainty ; when their claims

clashed, as they frequently had done, he was content
to defeat the attack or outwit the diplomacy of the
French king, but in the young Philip there was
growing up a far more formidable adversary and
one who could neither be hoodwinked nor driven
from the field without difficulty. For the time, however, Henry's relations with the young French king
were almost paternal. In the spring of 1180 Henry
intervened to reconcile Philip and his uncles of the
house of Blois, and in July of the following year he
patched up a peace between Philip and his wife's
uncle, Count Philip of Flanders. This peace was
broken before the end of the year, when Count
Philip formed a coalition against the King of France,
and he might have fared badly if the younger Henry,
who, had remained in Normandy after his father had
gone back to England, had not come to the rescue.
Peace was again patched up between France and
Flanders by Henry in March 1182, and the two
Philips united with Henry in intervening on behalf
of the latter's son-in-law, Henry the Lion of Saxony,
who had incurred the enmity of the Emperor Frederic
and had been sentenced to seven years' banishment.
As a result of this intervention the duke's sentence
was substantially reduced, and when he came to
Normandy with his wife and children he was
warmly welcomed and liberally provided for by
Henry.

Conspicuous as was Henry's success in dealing
with foreign princes, his failure when dealing

with his own sons was equally conspicuous. He could act as peacemaker between France and Flanders, but from 1176 onwards his sons were continually at war, sometimes assisting one another to suppress rebellious vassals, at other times quarrelling among themselves. Richard in particular was continually fighting in Poitou, where his arrogance and licentiousness had made him extremely unpopular with his subjects. Matters came to a crisis early in 1183, when, upon Richard's refusing to do homage for Poitou to the younger Henry, the latter with his brother Geoffrey joined the discontented Poitevins and made war upon Richard. King Henry came to the help of Richard and advanced to Limoges, where he had a narrow escape from being shot by his sons' soldiers. The rebellious princes, relying upon their father's affection, obtained a succession of truces which they broke without compunction whenever it suited their purpose, ill-treating his messengers and plundering his supporters. Geoffrey stripped the shrine of St. Martial at Limoges in order to pay his mercenaries, and the young king, finding his plans going astray, took an oath at that same shrine to go on crusade. His father endeavoured to persuade him to renounce the rash vow, but when he found him apparently intent upon the project generously promised to equip him. He repaid the generous offer by abandoning the scheme and indulging in a plundering foray, stripping the monastery of Grammont, the one religious house for which his father had displayed an affection. Towards the end of May 1183 the young king fell ill, but this did not deter him from sacking the famous shrine of Roquemadour. On his way back from this sacrilegious exploit he was obliged to stop at Martel, as his fever had much increased and soon developed into dysentery. Realising that it was likely to end in death he sent for his father, but Henry, naturally suspecting a trap, would not come, though he sent a sapphire ring to his son as a token of his affection, and possibly with the hope that the mystic curative qualities of that precious stone might prove beneficial. On 11th June the young man died, expressing a pious penitence which would have been more edifying had it been displayed earlier, and commissioning the faithful William Marshal, who had just been recalled to his court after an undeserved period of exile, to perform for him the two years' crusade which he had sworn to undertake.

The death of the unfilial and unprincipled Henry had followed so close upon his sacrilegious spoliation of St. Amadour that it might well have been considered a divine judgment, and it is almost incredible that even his most devoted partisans could have proclaimed him a saint; yet such was the case, and a few audacious and imaginative adherents even asserted that miracles had been wrought by him. His liberality, good fellowship, and manly courage, which showed itself in his addiction to the tournament, a form of sport so far from saintly that

L

it was under the papal ban, had made him friends who mourned his loss ; a still larger number regretted the removal of a tool so useful for undermining the influence of the hated King of England. The one man who sorrowed for him most sincerely was the father against whom he had sinned so persistently.

Within a month of the young king's death the rebellion which he had fomented was at an end. During the latter half of 1183 Henry appears to have made an uneventful tour through his continental dominions, but in the spring of 1184 we find him negotiating for the re-marriage of the Count of Flanders, sending his own royal yacht to fetch the bride, a daughter of the King of Portugal, and conducting her from La Rochelle to the Flemish border. And, more or less as the result of this marriage, we find him called upon to interfere once more between the King of France and the Count of Flanders to procure peace. Immediately afterwards, on 10th June 1184, Henry crossed once more to England, after an absence of two years. The next six months were largely taken up with the choice of a successor to Archbishop Richard, who had died in the preceding February. At last, after several names had been suggested by the Canterbury monks only to be rejected by the king, Bishop Baldwin of Worcester was elected on 16th December.

The year 1185 opened with the arrival at Canterbury of Heraclius, Patriarch of Jerusalem, charged

by Baldwin, the head of the tottering kingdom of
Jerusalem, with an appeal to Henry for help. On
18th March Henry gave formal audience to Heraclius,
who offered him the keys of the Holy Sepulchre and
the crown of Jerusalem, and produced a letter from
the pope urging a new crusade. By the advice of
his council Henry declared his inability to go in
person, and he also declined to accept the crown
for any of his sons, but he promised assistance in
men and money, and large numbers of his nobles
took the cross. A month later the king and the
patriarch passed over together into Normandy, and
on 1st May they had an interview with King Philip
of France, who took up the same line as Henry had
done, so that Heraclius had to return to his master
with the promise indeed of assistance, but disappointed in his hopes of obtaining an influential
leader. As soon as the interview was over Henry
had to turn his attention to his quarrelsome son
Richard. Untaught by experience, the king had
continued to provoke his sons against one another
and against himself, striving to wrest Aquitaine from
Richard for the benefit of John and then setting
John and Geoffrey to fight their elder brother ; this
quarrel had been composed for a time, but Richard
was now attacking the lands of his brother Geoffrey,
and in order to quiet him Henry sent for Queen
Eleanor, the rightful owner of Poitou, and forced
Richard to surrender the province into his mother's
hands. This had the desired effect of restoring

order, and in August 1186 Geoffrey was killed in a tournament at Paris, regretted by none except his father and Philip of France.

In May 1186 Henry, who was an inveterate matchmaker, had arranged for the marriage of King William of Scotland with his cousin Ermengarde, daughter of Richard, Viscount of Beaumont. The marriage took place at Woodstock on 5th September, Henry's wedding present taking the shape of the Castle of Edinburgh; but before it was celebrated the two kings had marched north together, in July, and compelled Ronald, son of Uctred, the usurping Lord of Galloway, to submit to Henry's judgment. But while Henry's relations with his old adversary of Scotland were thus satisfactory there was growing friction between him and Philip of France. The questions of the dower due to the young king's widow, Margaret, and of the marriage of Philip's other sister Alais to Richard, had been debated with acrimony on several occasions, and the action of the English Constable of Gisors in destroying a fortress in process of erection on the French border and killing the son of the French knight in charge of the work, in October 1186, had further exasperated Philip. For the time the storm blew over, but in May 1187, after an ineffective endeavour to come to terms with Philip, Henry prepared for war. The French king besieged Richard and John at Château-roux and Henry had to come to their rescue, but a pitched battle was avoided by the interposition of

Pope Urban III., whose anxiety for the fate of
Palestine made him particularly desirous of peace
in Europe, and a truce for two years was agreed
upon on 23rd June. Immediately afterwards Philip
began to cultivate Richard's friendship, hoping to
use him against his father, as he had done young
Henry and Geoffrey. Richard swallowed the bait
and went off with Philip, living for some time in the
closest intimacy with him, ignoring his father's remonstrances, and even plundering his treasury at
Chinon ; but after a while he came to a better mind
and returned to his allegiance.

In January 1188 Henry was preparing to return
to England, when Philip threatened to invade
Normandy unless the marriage of his sister Alais
and Richard were celebrated at once and the fortress
of Gisors surrendered to France. Henry at once
proceeded to meet him at the usual place, a great elm
standing on the borders of France and Normandy
near Gisors. Little progress was made in the negotiations until the arrival of the Archbishop of Tyre,
who preached a stirring sermon on the misfortunes
of Palestine, recounting the capture of King Guy
and the True Cross by Saladin in July 1187—a disaster which caused the death of Pope Urban III.—and
the fall of Jerusalem in the following October. His
hearers were so moved that almost with one accord
they vowed to go upon crusade, Henry and Philip
setting the example and putting aside all their
differences. So great were the numbers of those

that took the cross that it was needful to adopt
badges to distinguish the different nationalities,
the French wearing red crosses, the followers of the
English king white crosses, and the Flemings green.
Henry at once issued orders at Le Mans for the
collection of a tithe to be levied throughout all his
continental dominions. All persons who did not go
to the crusade themselves were to give a tenth of their
goods, and arrangements were made for ensuring
that none should evade his duty. Those who were
willing to serve in person might take the tithes of
their men and lands for their own equipment. As
soon as this ordinance had been published Henry
hastened to England, landing at Winchester on
30th January. A fortnight later a council was held
at Geddington, when the ordinance for the collection
of the crusading tithe, usually known as the Saladin
tithe, was made applicable to England. The King
of Scotland was urged to follow his suzerain's lead,
and Archbishop Baldwin was sent to preach the
crusade in Wales, accompanied by Gerald de Barri,
who has left an account of the mission containing
many interesting details of Welsh topography and
history and a very full appreciation of the services
rendered by Gerald himself.

Meanwhile Richard, who had taken the cross the
previous year in Brittany, was indulging in a little
war with the Count of Toulouse with considerable
success. Philip, who appears to have incited
Richard to action in order to pick a further quarrel

with Henry, now complained to the latter of his
son's conduct, and in June invaded Berry, capturing
Châteauroux and other places. Henry crossed once
more, for the last time, to Normandy, to find that
Richard had driven Philip out of Berry. After some
desultory border raiding a conference was arranged
between the two kings at the historic elm by Gisors.
Neither side would accede to the demands of the
other, and after a proposal to settle the dispute by
battle between four picked champions from either
side had been rejected, preparations were made to
resume the campaign. Some of the French troops,
irritated at the sight of the English resting in comfort
in the shade of the elm while they themselves were
out in the heat, cut down the famous tree. Philip
was annoyed at the spiteful vandalism, and Henry
vowed to revenge the elm.

For the moment no fighting took place ; the Counts
of Flanders and of Blois and other French nobles
declining to serve any longer against Christians when
their arms were so badly needed in Palestine, Philip
was obliged to disband his forces, and Henry did
likewise, giving, however, secret orders for their
reassembly at Paccy. Thence he sent them across
the French border to ravage the district round
Mantes, while Richard operated further south from
Châteauroux. King Henry took little active part
in this campaign, as he had been taken ill at Chinon
early in the autumn. A meeting of the kings at
Châtillon in October came to nothing, and Philip

began to tamper with Richard's unstable fidelity.
A promise that he should have Anjou, Touraine and
Maine in reward for deserting his father speedily
brought Richard over to Philip's side, and the latter
then arranged for a fresh conference with Henry at
Bonmoulins on 18th November.   Richard and Philip
arrived together, and though the former explained
to his father that his meeting with the French king
on the way was quite accidental, Henry's incredulity
and alarm were soon justified.   Philip, after proposing
a mutual retrocession of all territories taken during
the recent campaign, again demanded the marriage
of Richard and Alais, the cession to Richard of
Anjou, Touraine and Maine, and his acknowledgment
as Henry's heir.   King Henry refused these last
demands, and Richard angrily flung down his sword
and did homage to Philip for the three provinces
which his father had refused him.

A truce had been agreed upon to last until 13th
January 1189, but with its expiration Philip and
Richard renewed the attack.   Henry, whose health
had completely broken down, was laid up at Le
Mans during the spring, and from there he sent
William Marshal and the Archdeacon of Hereford
to Paris to negotiate with King Philip ; but by the
efforts of Richard and his wily minister, William
Longchamp, their endeavours were brought to
nought.   A slight improvement in his health enabled
Henry to meet his opponents in person on 28th May
at La Ferté Bernard, where Richard's demand that

his brother John should go on crusade was met by Henry not merely with a direct negative but with the suggestion that John should marry Alais and have the provinces which Richard claimed. This, while exasperating Richard still more completely, did not appeal to Philip, and, in spite of the efforts of the legate, Cardinal John of Anagni, who threatened to lay his dominions under an interdict if he did not make peace, the French king resumed the campaign with vigour, and after several smaller successes appeared before Le Mans on 12th June. The bridges across the Sarthe had been broken down and the known fords blocked with sharp stakes, but the French cavalry, sounding the river with their spears, found a place where they could cross and caught the English by surprise. During the sharp fighting that ensued outside the town Stephen of Tours, the governor of the town, set fire to a suburb whose buildings would have afforded dangerous cover for the assailants. Unfortunately the wind suddenly shifted and, blowing strongly, drove the flames into the city, which itself caught fire in several places. Realising the desperate nature of their position King Henry and his knights sought safety in flight. They were pursued by a force of cavalry under the leadership of Richard, who was some way in advance of his followers and rapidly overtaking the king when William Marshal turned upon him. Count Richard had for some reason thrown aside his defensive armour, and, seeing himself at the Marshal's mercy,

called to him not to kill him. " Not I ! the devil
may kill you ! " retorted the knight, and, lowering
his lance, he struck the count's horse dead, bringing
its rider to the ground.   Richard at once called off
his men and abandoned the pursuit, and Henry,
pausing for a while on a little hill and looking back
upon his beloved native town in flames, burst into a
flood of furious blasphemy, vowing that as God had
cheated him of the place which he loved better than
all others so he would cheat God of his soul.

With Henry were his son John and his illegitimate
son Geoffrey. This Geoffrey, the only one of Henry's
sons worthy of the name, was born about 1153, his
mother being a woman of humble position ; [1] he was
devoted to his father and, as bishop-elect of Lincoln,
had taken a vigorous part in the suppression of the
rebellion of 1173–4. Resigning the see of Lincoln
in 1181 he became chancellor, in which office he was
in constant attendance upon the king. At Le Mans
he fought valiantly with fire and foe, and now that
the fugitives had reached Fresnai he proposed to
spend the night outside the castle so as to bear the
brunt of any attack that might be made. To this
Henry would not assent, and it was Geoffrey's cloak
that covered the weary king when he flung himself
down, clothed as he was, for the night. Next day,
refusing the advice of his barons to fall back on

---

[1] She was apparently still alive in 1181, when a small allowance
was made her, the sum of 66s. 8d. paid " matri G. cancellarii ad eam
sustentandam " appearing amongst the charges on the bishopric of
Lincoln.

SEAL OF GEOFFREY THE BASTARD AS BISHOP ELECT
OF LINCOLN (⸸)

SEAL OF JOHN AS COUNT OF MORTAIN (⸸)

Normandy, Henry sent Geoffrey with almost all his forces to Alençon, himself making his way towards Chinon. John now took the opportunity of deserting his father, although Henry had just shown his partiality for him by making the seneschal of Normandy and Earl William de Mandeville swear that in the event of his death they would only give up the castles of Normandy to John and to none other. Geoffrey, his brother, base in birth but not in nature, as soon as he had discharged his commission spurred back to join his royal father, whose illness, aggravated by the strain and grief of the last few days, had entered upon its final stage.

Meanwhile Philip, carrying everything before him, had reached Tours on 30th June. There he received a mission from the Count of Flanders, the Archbishop of Rheims, and the Duke of Burgundy, urging him to come to terms with Henry. Tours was captured on 3rd July, and next day King Henry agreed to a meeting at a house of Templars not far from Colombier, near Azai, but when Henry reached the spot and dismounted he found that his legs would not support him, and his agony was such that he was obliged to lie down. King Philip and Richard on their arrival, not finding Henry, denounced his illness as a feint, and it was not until the king rode up, supported on his horse by his attendants, that they realised that he was dying. Philip courteously spread a cloak upon the ground and bade him be seated, but his indomitable spirit

would not allow him to display so much weakness.
He had come prepared to accept any terms, to make
any concessions, but with the full intention, if he
lived, of winning all back by the power of the sword.
Philip's terms, considering the hopeless position of
his adversary, were not ungenerous. Henry had to
surrender all claims to Auvergne and to do homage
to Philip for his continental dominions ; Alais was
to be taken from his custody and married to Richard,
who was to be recognised as his father's heir and to
receive the fealty of his barons. Moreover, all those
who had joined Richard during the war were to
remain his men and not to return to their allegiance
to Henry. Finally, Henry was to pay 20,000 marks
to the French king, and the agreement for a common
crusade was renewed, Lent 1190 being named as the
date and Vézelay as the rendezvous. At the end
of the interview Henry had to give his son the formal
kiss of peace, but as he did so he muttered, " May God
grant that I live long enough to take my revenge
upon you," a threat at which Richard openly jested
to his friends.

Henry returned from Colombier to Chinon, and as
he lay upon his deathbed the list of those who had
deserted him and sworn allegiance to Richard was
brought in. He bade the bearer read out the names,
but when the first name of all proved to be his best-
loved son, John, for whom he had done so much,
he stopped the reader, saying, " It is enough ! Now
let come what may ! " Broken-hearted and racked

with pain the great king lingered on for two days, mut-
tering in his delirium "Shame on a conquered king!"
and cursing his sons. The sole redeeming feature
of these last days was the unremitting tenderness
with which Geoffrey nursed his father, who repaid
his affectionate care with words of loving praise,
giving him at the last his royal signet ring engraved
with his symbol, a leopard.[1] Yet even Geoffrey
seems to have been absent at the moment that his
father passed away, and the few servants who were
there, seizing the opportunity to lay hands on everything portable that was worth taking, left the king's
body lying half naked and uncared for, till one
William Trihan, known only to history for this good
act, placed over his royal master his cloak, appro-
priately one of the short Angevin cloaks, the introduction of which into England had earned Henry
the nickname of " Courtmantel."

Thus, on 6th July 1189, died Henry II.

Next day the dead king was carried to Fontevrault,
where, in the church of the great nunnery, his body
lay for a time in state. Hither came Richard, now
in his turn king; for a while he stood and gazed
at the stern uncovered face of his father, then,
kneeling for a brief moment in prayer, rose, and

---

[1] It is interesting to observe that Matthew Paris assigns to the
young king Henry a shield of arms,—per pale gules and sable, three
golden leopards; *Chron. Maj.* (Rolls Ser.), vi. 473. This bears
every mark of being an exceptionally early instance of differencing,
and makes it more than probable that Henry II. bore the red shield
with the three golden leopards, which has ever since been the arms
of England.

calling William Marshal and Maurice de Craon to
him, strode out of the church. In a few words he
showed that he bore no ill-will towards his father's
loyal adherents and then departed, to return next
day for the funeral. Henry had never cared much
for the outward pomp and circumstance of kings,
and such emblems of royalty as he may have had
with him in his last days seem to have been either
lost at Le Mans or stolen at the time of his death.
And so when he was being robed for burial it was with
difficulty that the royal insignia of crown, ring and
sceptre could be improvised, and he who had been
the greatest of the princes of Europe was laid to
rest with less ceremonial splendour than many an
obscure vassal.

TOMB OF HENRY II AT FONTEVRAULT

CHAPTER IX

THE reign of Henry II. is of particular importance
in English constitutional and legal history. It was
a period of evolution, of crystallisation, a period of
transition. As in architecture we have at this time
the transition from Norman, or Romanesque, to
Gothic, so we have the transition from oral tradition
and custom to written law and formula. As the
Saxon blood was blending with the Norman to form
the English people, so Saxon law was assimilating
Roman law and the theories of the Canonists to
form English law. The genius of Henry lay rather
in organisation than in initiative. Possessing an
innate love of justice and an instructed appreciation
of legal forms, he set himself to evolve method and
order from the somewhat chaotic confusion of con-
flicting customs. Under his hand the young plant
of English law was pruned, trained, and bent in the
direction in which it was to grow during the suc-
ceeding centuries. His natural inclination for the
work was doubtless whetted by the twofold consideration that every extension of the central royal
jurisdiction involved a diminution of local feudal

jurisdiction and that increase of legal control implied increase of revenue. The personal part played by the king in the administration of the law was striking. Constantly we find him sitting in a judicial capacity, following with more or less patience the involved arguments of the advocates, inspecting charters in dispute, criticising them shrewdly and impartially, and exhibiting a legal acumen which proved that he was worthy, apart from his rank, to preside over the ultimate court of appeal.[1] The strong arm of the law could hardly be invoked without his aid, and the slow foot of justice could only be hastened with his assistance. And for such assistance payment must be made. Henry was, indeed, notorious as a "seller of justice"; but if the commodity was expensive it was at least the best of its kind, and there is a profound gulf between the selling of justice and of injustice. A bribe might be required to set the machine of the law in motion, but it would be unavailing to divert its course when once started. When John le Viel, a wealthy citizen of London, was convicted of taking part in a series of outrages which culminated in the murder of Earl Ferrers' brother in 1177, his offer of 500 marks to the king

[1] As for instance in the case of the disputed privileges of the abbey of St. Alban's, when his examination of their charters and his comments thereon showed remarkable painstaking ability : *Gesta Abbatum S. Albani* (Rolls Ser.) i. 145–155. Another case, reported in still greater detail, is the suit between the Bishop of Chichester and the Abbot of Battle : *Chron. of Battle Abbey* (ed. Lower), 78–115. For an instance of the king's appreciation of legal technicalities, see *ibid.*, 182.

gained him no reprieve and he suffered the death penalty with his humbler and poorer accomplices.

It is partly owing to the personal predominance of the king as law-giver that exact dates and details of the institution or formal adoption of certain methods of legal procedure are hard to ascertain. A verbal instruction or a few written lines to the justiciar would be enough to establish a formula which would rapidly become a commonplace of law without exciting comment from any chronicler. There are, however, some four or five occasions on which a definite code of laws or regulations was published and duly recorded. The first of these was the code drawn up in 1164 to define the relations of Church and State. The circumstances in which these " Constitutions of Clarendon " were drawn up have already been considered. They were drawn up definitely as representing the rules in force in the time of Henry I., and it would seem that for the most part they could fairly claim this antiquity, though their continuity had been broken by the disorder of Stephen's reign. That they lost something of their elasticity and became more pronouncedly favourable to the secular courts when they were reduced to writing can hardly be doubted, and that there was some small amount of actual innovation is highly probable, but it is as compiler rather than author that the name of Henry II. should be associated with the Constitutions of Clarendon.

By these Constitutions it was asserted (cap. 1)

M

that all actions concerning the advowsons of churches should be heard in the king's court,[1] even if both parties were clerks, and that (cap. 2) the king's consent must be obtained before any church held in fee of the crown could be granted in perpetuity. By a further assertion of the royal proprietary rights (cap. 12) the king claimed to have the custody and control of all sees, and of such monasteries as were in the patronage of the crown, during their vacancies, and to determine when their new heads should be elected. Whatever may be said against this claim morally—and it certainly gave the king every inducement to prolong such vacancies and leave a wealthy see or abbey headless—it was undoubtedly a custom of respectable antiquity, based presumably on analogy with the king's feudal right to the custody of the lands of his lay tenants-in-chief during the minority of their heirs. The identity of status of lay and ecclesiastical tenants was insisted upon in the order (cap. 11) that prelates and beneficed clergy who held of the king in chief should hold their lands as baronies and perform the services due therefrom, including the duty of sitting as judges on the Bench with the lay barons, save that they should not take part in pronouncing sentence of death or mutilation.

Besides pleas of advowsons all pleas of debt were now removed from the ecclesiastical courts (cap. 15),

---

[1] The Pipe Roll for 31 Henry II. records a fine of 500 marks imposed on the Bishop of Durham for holding a plea touching the advowson of a church in Court Christian.

even when involving breach of oath. A third class
of actions, those concerned with lands said to be
granted in alms to churches, involved a more
elaborate procedure (cap. 9). If a piece of land
were claimed by a clerk as belonging to his church
and by a layman as belonging to his lay fee the
question was first to be referred to a jury of twelve
men of good standing; if they decided that the
land was held in alms the case should be tried in
the ecclesiastical court, but if the contrary, then in
the king's court. The appearance of this jury of
twelve is very important, and it occurs again in the
Constitutions. Certain moral offences were ad-
mittedly the province of the Court Christian, but it
was common knowledge that the archdeacons and
their officials, whether from lack of legal training or
of charity, accepted accusations on very insufficient
evidence ; it was therefore laid down (cap. 6) that
such accusations ought not to be made against
laymen unless supported by responsible witnesses ;
but in cases where witnesses dare not come forward,
owing to the rank or power of the accused, a jury
of twelve men of good standing might be summoned
to inquire into the truth of the accusations.

In these two instances of the appointment of
juries we have almost certainly innovations, and it is
to Henry II. that we must attribute the institution of
the trial by jury. It must be borne in mind that
just as these twelve jurors differed in everything
but number from the Anglo-Saxon " doomsmen,"

whose office was to give sentence, so they also differed from the modern jury. The modern juryman is supposed to start with a completely open mind, and indeed in America even a remote and superficial knowledge of the nature of the case to be tried has been considered a disqualification ; but the medieval jurors were men chosen for their knowledge of the matter in dispute ; they were witnesses—not witnesses for the prosecution or for the defence, but, being summoned by an impartial authority, witnesses for the truth ; they answered the questions put to them in the light of their personal knowledge and not as a result of deductions from the deliberately misleading arguments of rival advocates. The evolution and progress of legal procedure is always interesting, and particularly so in the case of the peculiarly English institution of the jury. The occasional appointment of juries of inquest to settle special points may, of course, be traced back for generations, but the definite establishment of the jury as a legal instrument dates from the reign of Henry II.

The claims of the spiritual courts were complicated by possessing a double basis ; on the one hand they claimed all actions which could in any way be held to be concerned with morals or with the property of the Church, and on the other they claimed jurisdiction over all persons who had been admitted to the ranks of the clergy. While admitting the theory of clerical exemption in criminal cases Henry endeavoured to neutralise it in practice. The suggested compromise, which was the chief bone of contention between him and the Church party, was (cap. 3) that an accused clerk should be summoned before the king's court, and if a *primâ facie* case were made out against him he should be remitted to the bishop's court for fuller trial and sentence, the proceedings being watched by one of the royal officials. If convicted he should *ipso facto* forfeit the Church's protection and become amenable to the common law. This latter proviso had to be abandoned, but within about a century of the birth of the Constitutions the royal courts had established their right to pronounce upon the guilt of an accused clerk before handing him over to the ecclesiastical court. While the Church was claiming exemption from lay justice it was natural that an endeavour should be made in retaliation to limit the scope of the Church's sentence, and accordingly it was ordered (cap. 7) that no tenant-in-chief or royal officer should be excommunicated without the king's permission, and a similar protection was extended (cap. 10) to all persons dwelling in a royal borough, castle, or manor. In both cases it was expressly stated that the king or his officials would endeavour to compel the offender to make satisfaction, so obviating the necessity for excommunication, and indeed it was laid down (cap. 13) that the royal and ecclesiastical courts should give one another mutual assistance in bringing offenders to book.

A further blow was aimed at clerical independence

by the regulation (cap. 8) that there should be
appeals from the archdeacon's court to that of the
bishop and thence to that of the archbishop, but that
appeal from the archbishop's court should be to the
king's court and not to Rome without royal consent.
To prevent this rule being broken Henry maintained
(cap. 4) that prelates and beneficed clergy had no
right to leave the country without royal licence, and
that in any case they must swear to do nothing to
the prejudice of king or realm during their absence.
The supremacy of the pope, however, proved to be
too firmly rooted in the minds of the clergy, and
these articles had to be dropped, Henry himself
during the Becket controversy being obliged to resort
to constant appeals and counter-appeals to the
papal court

During the seven years' struggle with Becket
which followed the promulgation of the Constitutions of Clarendon, Henry did not neglect the cause
of legal reform, and early in 1166 he issued an
important series of injunctions known as the Assize
of Clarendon. These injunctions, turning upon the
existence of a system of itinerant justices, whose
presence in all parts of the country at frequent
intervals they take for granted, prove that the
custom of sending commissions of judges on circuit,
which had been inaugurated by Henry I., but had
fallen almost out of use, and certainly out of all
regularity, under Stephen, had been restored by
Henry II. The evidence of the Pipe Rolls shows

that during the early years of the reign most of these
" eyres," or itinerant courts, were held by the leading
royal officers, such as the chancellor, the justiciar, or
the Earl of Essex, acting singly or together, but in
1176 the king divided the whole country into six
circuits and appointed three justices to each circuit.
For some reason this scheme did not work well,
possibly from an excess of zeal and self-importance
on the part of the justices, and in 1179 Henry re-
voked these appointments and constituted a central
royal court of five justices ; subsidiary to this permanent court he established four circuits, the commission for each circuit being five judges, though,
by an apparent contradiction, the commissioners for
the northern circuit were the officers of the permanent central court. The arrangement of the
circuits varied from time to time and constant
changes were made in the personnel of the judges,
but the main features of itinerant courts with a
permanent central court above them became fixed.
From the central court there was appeal in cases
of difficulty to the king and council.[1] As we have
already said, Henry took a large personal share in
the administration of justice, but he acted strictly
within constitutional limits, and it was always the
council that pronounced the sentence, though the
influence of the king's expressed opinion would
naturally be paramount.

[1] An instance of a difficult case being referred by the justiciar to
King Henry occurs in the *Chron. Mon. de Abingdon* (Rolls Ser.), ii. 229.

By the Assize of Clarendon it was ordered that the sheriffs and itinerant justices should make careful search for evil-doers throughout the country. Twelve men of good standing from each hundred and four from each township were to declare on oath what men in their district were known or suspected to be robbers, murderers, thieves, or harbourers of bad characters. All such were at once to be arrested and brought before the nearest justice and compelled to purge themselves by the ordeal of water. In this ordeal the accused was bound hand and foot and thrown into a pond or pit, of which the water had previously been consecrated by a priest.[1] If the water rejected him, so that he floated, he was considered guilty, his foot was struck off and his goods were forfeited to the king; but if the water received him and he sank he was dragged to land and his innocence was held to have been proved. But a sceptical feeling towards the ordeal was growing up, and the Assize ordered that if the repute of the accused were notoriously bad and the accusations against him well sustained, then, even if he acquitted himself by the ordeal, he should be banished

[1] Instances of the blessing of the ordeal pits occur in the Pipe Rolls. In 1166, for instance, 10s. was paid to two priests for blessing the pits (fossarum) at Bury St. Edmunds, and in Wiltshire 5s. was paid for preparing the pools (polis) for the ordeal of thieves, and 20s. to priests for blessing the same pools. As early as 1158 the sheriff of Wiltshire accounted for making " the pools of the moneyers," and in 1175 in Hampshire there were payments made for " blessing the ordeal pits (fossis iuisse), and the cost of doing justice on the peasants who burnt their lord."

from the country, being bound to leave England within a week, or as soon after as the wind would serve.

By reserving all cases of this type to the jurisdiction of the king's courts and by authorising the sheriffs to enter any " liberty " or honour for the purposes of arresting criminals or of supervising the police organisation of frank pledges a severe blow was struck at the private feudal courts, and, incidentally, the security of the law-abiding populace was much increased. To strengthen this security yet more the king gave orders for the erection of gaols in every county and for the compilation of lists of fugitive criminals. No unknown wayfarer or vagabond might stay for more than one night in any borough unless he or his horse fell ill, and all newcomers settling in any county had to find sureties for their appearance before the justices, while a final haven of refuge was closed to the fugitive by the rule that no religious house should receive into its fellowship any man of the lower class (*de minuto populo*) without inquiry into his antecedents.

It is probably to this same year, 1166, that we may assign the Assize of Novel Disseisin, by which possession became not merely nine-tenths of the law but the law itself. Under this assize any person who was seised, or possessed, of a freehold and was ejected therefrom, or disseised, without a previous decision of the court, might recover his seisin by an action before the king's court, without regard to the goodness of his original title. There is some

reason to believe that this theory of the right of
the actual possessor to remain in possession until
the claimant had proved his better right to the
property was recognised in the previous reign, but
it was under Henry II. that it took definite form as
a fixed method of legal procedure which formed the
basis of innumerable actions in later times. About
this same date, too, we find evolving another legal
form which was to play a very important part in the
history of the conveyance of land. It is self-evident
that from time to time the parties concerned in a
suit before the king's court might find it to their
mutual advantage to come to a compromise. As this
would involve the abandoning of the suit, probably
depriving the king of certain perquisites of justice
and certainly rendering nugatory the trouble taken
by the justices over the preliminaries of the trial,
the king's leave to compromise had to be purchased,
and frequently the terms of the agreement were
submitted to him for confirmation. To begin with,
these agreements, which from their putting an end
to the suit were called " final concords " or " fines,"
would be drawn up casually, expressing each particular composition in such phrases as seemed most
convenient, but the Justiciar Glanville, writing at
the end of Henry's reign, lays down a definite
formula to be used in drawing up a Fine, and this
formula can be traced back to 1172 and occurs,
with slight variations, as early as 1163,[1] though

[1] *Engl. Hist. Rev.*, xxv. 709.

instances before 1180 are rare. When these Fines acquired the recognised status of legal formulæ steps were taken to preserve official copies of them, and as soon as it was realised that the execution of a Fine was the surest way of securing a permanent record of a conveyance of land, or similar deed, it became the practice to bring fictitious actions with the express intention of compromising them and executing Fines. The Fine was, therefore, at a later date almost invariably the termination of a fictitious suit, but there is no reason to believe that this was so in the time of Henry II. to any great extent, and though we owe to him the formula of the Fine it remained in his time a genuine act of compromise, and incidentally a considerable source of revenue.

The administration of the Assize of Clarendon, especially of those portions concerned with forfeitures and pecuniary penalties, seems to have given rise to much complaint. The sheriffs were said on the one hand to have used their power to extort more than was due and on the other hand to have paid into the exchequer less than was due. Further rumours of peculation in connection with the aid for the marriage of the king's daughter in 1168 having reached Henry's ears, he suspended all the sheriffs in 1170, and ordered a careful and minute inquiry into the whole question. All moneys paid to sheriffs and other officials, or to magnates and their stewards, during the past four years, were to be set down, with a notice whether they were demanded with lawful warrant or without. The value of the goods of convicted or fugitive felons and the amounts paid towards the marriage aid were also to be returned, and note was to be made of any bribes accepted by the sheriffs or hush-money given by them. The inquiry was also to extend to breaches of the Forest Law and the conduct of the officials administering it. The only fragments of the returns [1] to this inquiry that are known to have survived throw little light on the general conduct of the sheriffs and their subordinates, though they illustrate the truth that taxation always soaks through to the lowest stratum of society. Although taxation under Henry did not fall with nearly so direct and crushing a force upon the poor as under King Louis in France, the large sums extorted from the English magnates had naturally to be raised by them in part from their poorer tenants, and if the king expected his lords to make large " gifts " of money to him it was natural that they should in turn impress upon their subjects the duty of giving " willingly " to them.

One immediate result of this inquiry of 1170 was the substitution of men from the ranks of the exchequer and court officials in place of local magnates as sheriffs. The change was a wise one, increasing

---

[1] The fragmentary return to the Inquest of Sheriffs made from the Earl of Arundel's lands in Norfolk has been printed as an appendix to the *Red Book of the Exchequer* in the Rolls Series, but was first identified by Mr. Round.

the skill of administration and reducing the risk of
extortion and undue use of influence. The continuous undermining of the baronial authority, of
which this was but one more instance, had a double
effect at the time of the young king's rebellion in
1173 ; on the one hand it drove the more intolerant
nobles to take up arms against King Henry, but on
the other it put in the king's hand a powerful organisation controlled by loyal officials, whose prospects
were bound up with his own and supported by the
mass of the people, who had every reason to appreciate his rule and to fear the victory of the feudal
reactionaries. After the rebellion had quieted down
Henry issued, at Northampton in 1176, an assize of
wider scope than any other of his reign. The decrees
of the Assize of Clarendon were repeated but re-
enforced ; forgery and arson were added to the
Pleas of the Crown about which inquiry was to be
made, and the convicted felon was to lose a hand
as well as a foot. Returns were to be made of the
escheats, churches, and heiresses who were in the
king's gift, and the justices were to try actions brought
under the Assize of Novel Disscisin and were also
given control of cases concerned with as little as
half a knight's fee. Finally, an important regulation was laid down that if a free tenant died his son
and heir should at once have such seisin of the freehold as his father had at the time of his death, and
the widow should have her dower. If the lord of
the fee did not admit the heir of the freehold the

justices should cause an inquest to be made by the
jury of twelve men which had now become so integral
a part of legal procedure, and if they found that the
father had died seised the heir should recover possession. In this we have clearly the first enuncia-
tion of the Assize of Mort d'Ancestor, which in course
of time was extended from the direct to the more
remote degrees of kindred.

The work begun by the Assizes of Novel Disseisin
and Mort d'Ancestor was brought to a logical com-
pletion in 1179 by the institution of the Grand Assize.
By this assize any action concerning a freehold
could be transferred from the manorial to the royal
court. The demandant in the lower court was
bound, as of old, to offer to prove his claim by the
judicial duel, a clumsy process entailing endless
delays and expense and the humiliation, if not
death, of the defeated party, and often ending in a
way clearly contrary to justice. Now, by this new
regulation, the tenant when challenged might " put
himself upon the assize " ; the demandant would
then sue a writ in the king's court, four knights
would be appointed to elect a jury of twelve knights,
or country gentlemen as we should call them, associated with the district in which the disputed land
lay. The jury had then to state from their own
knowledge, or from what their fathers had told
them, which of the two parties had the better claim
to the land. If any of the jury did not know anything of the matter they were discharged and others

put in their place, and if the knights were divided in opinion their numbers were increased until twelve decided in favour of one party. Knowing, as we do from the Plea Rolls of the next reign, how protracted a suit might be under this assize, we can appreciate from Glanville's encomium on the comparative rapidity of the process how interminable must have been the proceedings under the old methods. It was not only a great extension of the influence of the king's court, but was also a victory for common sense and sound law, and the absurd and illogical ordeal by battle rapidly fell into disuse, though it was not actually repealed in English law until 1819 and is still retained for the settlement of international quarrels.

The Grand Assize of 1179 is the last definite reform of Common Law procedure that we can connect with Henry's name, but in 1184 he issued an Assize of the Forest. Under the Norman kings the doctrine of royal rights over those unreclaimed woodlands, moors, and heaths which were known as forests was rigorously asserted. Henry I., in particular, had so stretched his claims as to exercise jurisdiction over the sporting preserves of his barons, ignoring their rights and oppressing their tenants by the application of the arbitrary regulations of the Forest Law. Stephen had been compelled to relinquish all those forests which had been created by Henry I., and to confine the claims of the crown to those that were in existence at the time of the death of William

Rufus, but Henry II. had gradually reasserted his grandfather's claims, though not in their entirety. Henry himself was an ardent sportsman, finding in hunting and hawking an outlet for his ceaseless activity of spirit, and appears to have regarded poaching on the royal preserves as the most heinous of all offences. From the beginning of his reign justices from time to time toured the country inquiring into breaches of the Forest Law and mulcting the offenders, and we have seen how in 1176 he bled the whole country by a deliberate abuse of that same law, but it does not seem that any definite code was drawn up until the assize was published at Woodstock in 1184. Whether this was a stiffening of the laws in use, as is generally assumed, or a relaxation, or merely a codification, cannot be decided. In any case the laws, though severe, were less savage than those of Henry I. The technical details of the regulations touching the king's forests and his subjects' woods and coverts cannot here be dealt with, but some of the devices to stop poaching may be noticed. No one within the forest bounds might keep bows and arrows, dogs or hounds without licence ; hunting at night involved a year's imprisonment and a fine ; all large dogs (*mastivi*) within the forest districts were to be hambled, that is to say, lamed by cutting out the ball of the foot, to prevent their chasing the deer, and no tanner or white tawer might ply his trade within the forest bounds outside a borough. Finally every man above twelve

years of age within the forest district had to swear
to observe the laws ; this applied also to all clerks
holding lay fees, and in many ways the most notable
section of the assize is that which definitely asserts
the susceptibility of the clergy to the Forest Law
and authorises the royal officers to lay hands on
clerical offenders.

CHAPTER X

FINANCE

FINANCE plays as prominent a part in public as in private life, and the fortunes of a nation are as much built upon a money basis as those of an individual. This somewhat obvious truism is particularly applicable to the reign of Henry II., owing to the important share taken by hired mercenary soldiers in his numerous campaigns, the wealth at the king's disposal frequently enabling him to dispense with the service of disaffected or untrustworthy vassals. And the main source of this wealth was England, or at least it was from England that were drawn those extra supplies that formed the critical margin of safety, for while we hear constantly of treasure sent from England to the king or his ministers in Normandy we find no trace of any surplus from Henry's continental treasuries reaching the treasury at Winchester. Fortunately we possess the material for our examination in the series of revenue accounts known as the Pipe Rolls, complete from the second to the last year of the reign.

The treasury, with the controlling machinery of the exchequer, had been fully organised under Henry I., and an analysis by Sir James Ramsay of

the one surviving Pipe Roll of that king's reign,
that for the thirty-first year (1130), shows the total
royal revenue to have been about £27,000. During
the anarchy that prevailed under Stephen's nominal
sovereignty the organisation of the exchequer
virtually fell into abeyance. While there is no
evidence of Stephen having been at any time in
difficulties for lack of money, it is clear that his
permanent and assured revenues must have been
very small. The districts in which his power was
sufficiently established to ensure the collection of
the royal dues varied from time to time and at best
were limited, while their yield was still further
reduced by the lavish grants of crown demesnes
with which he had been compelled to purchase the
allegiance of powerful barons. Henry II., on coming
to the throne, had, as we have seen, resumed possession of the royal demesnes thus alienated, and he
also entrusted the re-organisation of the exchequer to
Nigel, Bishop of Ely. Order was soon restored, though
it was several years before we find the same elaboration
of the financial network as was exhibited in 1130.

A careful analysis of the Pipe Roll for 1156, the
first of the series, shows that the total amount of
the revenues dealt with, which exclude the issues
of the three northern counties, still at that time in
the hands of the King of Scotland, was in round
figures £21,650. But of this £6000 has to be de-
ducted for portions of the royal demesnes which had
been granted to various persons, and for payments

pardoned or remitted by the king. Another £2250
had not been paid and was still owing, a certain
proportion being bad debts. Of the remainder,
£9120 was paid into the treasury in cash and £4260
had been spent by the sheriffs and other accountants
on the king's behalf in payment of alms, repairs to
buildings, wages and miscellaneous purchases. The
actual revenue of this year may therefore be taken
as about £13,000, or rather less than half that of
Henry I. in 1130.

Turning now to the consideration of the sources of
revenue, the first is the farms (*firmæ*) of the various
counties and honours, these being fixed sums at
which the sheriffs of the counties or the farmers of
the honours compounded for the issues of the lands
under their control. Upon occasion a county might
for some reason be without a sheriff, in which case
one or more wardens (*custodes*) would be appointed,
and they would answer in detail for the issues and
receive payment in reward for their services. In some
cases the totals of these issues amount, as we should
expect, to more than the fixed farm, the difference
between the two sums being what the sheriff would
have for his labour. But occasionally, and notably
in the case of London,[1] the yield under *custodes* was
considerably less than under a sheriff. It is hardly
conceivable that the sheriff, in addition to the labour
and responsibility of his official duties, should have
been expected to make a loss over the render of his

[1] See Round, *Commune of London*, 229–233.

farm, but our knowledge of the methods by which the various moneys were collected before they reached the exchequer is too slight to enable us to explain this phenomenon. An incident which throws upon the question a light so uncertain as to render it almost more obscure occurred at the beginning of the Becket controversy. At a council held at Woodstock in 1163 the king demanded that a certain payment customarily made to the sheriffs from the lands of the counties under their control should in future be entered on the rolls and accounted for at the exchequer. Archbishop Becket rejected the demand, declaring that the payments in question were voluntary, that they depended upon the good conduct of the sheriffs, and that he would never consent to pay one penny on this account to the king. The chronicler who relates this incident at most length adds that the payment in question was two shillings from every hide, but this was almost certainly an error due to confusion with the Danegeld; the "sheriff's aid," about which the dispute arose, was not levied on any fixed basis but varied in different parts of the country.[1]

[1] In connection with the "sheriff's aid" there is an interesting entry in the *Chronicle of Abingdon* (ii. 230), which relates that a former abbot had granted the sheriff 100s. yearly to protect the interests of the abbey's tenants. The later sheriffs had continued to draw the money while doing nothing for it, and Abbot Ingulf refused to continue the payment, lest it should become established as a custom. The matter was brought before King Henry, who gave his decision in the abbot's favour. The survey of the manors belonging to the canons of St. Paul's in 1181 shows that the payments due to the sheriff from the different manors varied from 6d. to 4s. on the hide.

So far as we can see, the object of King Henry was to make the sheriffs more entirely dependent upon himself, drawing them into the position of the *custodes* as mere salaried officials of the exchequer; incidentally, no doubt, he hoped at the same time to obtain a substantial increase of revenue by appropriating the " aid." The objection voiced by Becket seems to have been based precisely on the king's wish to make the sheriffs responsible solely to himself; under the existing arrangement a sheriff who abused his authority ran the risk of losing the emoluments of his office, and even with this check these officials and their underlings not infrequently misused their power, extorting money from those under them and failing to account at the exchequer for money received. So notorious, indeed, did their maladministration become that, as we have seen, in 1170 Henry was driven to take summary action, removing all the sheriffs from office and appointing commissions to inquire into their conduct. Some of the officials thus removed were fined and very few were restored to their former position, but the new men appointed do not seem to have been greatly superior to their predecessors, and it is clear that whatever the sheriff lost or made over his farm he certainly possessed valuable perquisites, both legitimate and of doubtful legality.

The farms were the only fixed source of revenue, but an uncertain amount could always be relied upon from legal procedure (*placita*), fines inflicted for

breaches of either the Common or Forest Law,
amercements levied on hundreds, tithings, or townships for murders, payments made for leave to
compound a suit begun in the king's court, and
penalties due from the defeated party in a judicial
duel. For the most part the items under this head
were small, though in the aggregate their amount
was considerable, but not infrequently we find heavy
fines inflicted upon men of wealth, for which no
reason is given and which were in some cases, no
doubt, arbitrary acts of extortion on the king's part.
In 1165 Earl Hugh of Norfolk paid half of a fine of
1000 marks, while the Abbot of St. Edmunds, William
Cheyney, and two other East Anglican magnates were
amerced 200 marks apiece. That same year Hugh
de Mortimer was fined 500 marks, the Bishop of
Lincoln 400 marks, Ivo de Harcourt 300 marks, Ralf
de Cahaignes and Lefwin of York a like amount, the
Abbot of Westminster £100, and Abraham, the Jew
of London, £2000. The Jews, indeed, were a fruitful
source of income : their financial genius had enabled
them to concentrate most of the floating capital
of the country in their hands. They had almost
as much a monopoly of ready money as they had
of the trade of usury. In this latter respect their
monopoly was protected by the ban of the Church
directed against Christian usurers, and, safe from com-
petition, they lent their money at their own terms,
usually about 60 per cent., to litigants, ambitious
prelates, or impoverished monasteries, at one time

financing an unauthorised expedition to Ireland and at another assisting the king with large advances.[1] Henry was too sensible of their value to persecute, or to permit his subjects to persecute, the Jews, but he had no scruples in fining them arbitrarily enormous sums, which might have been crippling if they had ever paid more than a fraction of them, and in 1188, when he ordered his other subjects to pay a tenth of their goods towards the crusade, he made the Jews contribute a quarter instead of a tenth. In this latter case one of the London Jews was allowed to compound for his share of the subsidy by a payment of £200, of which half was to be paid, perhaps by the grim humour of the king, on the Sunday on which the canticle " Rejoice, O Jerusalem " is sung. It was in the previous year that the wealthiest of all the English Jews, the famous Aaron of Lincoln, had died, and by the law relating to usurers, whether Jew or Christian, his immense possessions, equal apparently to more than the yearly revenues of the crown, had fallen to the king, only to perish in great part beneath the waves of the Channel.

[1] The numerous references to Jews on the Pipe Rolls and in contemporary chronicles have been brought together in Jacobs' *The Jews of Angevin England*. Examples of their dealings with monastic houses may be found in Jocelin of Brakelond's *Chronicle*, relating to St. Edmund's Abbey, and in the *Gesta Abbatum* concerning St. Alban's, while an idea of their importance to the litigant in want of ready money for legal expenses may be gathered from Richard of Anstey's famous story of the costs of his lawsuit (translated in Hall's *Court Life of the Plantagenets*), in which he accounts for some seventeen different loans, amounting in all to £87, on which he paid £53 for usury.

If the death of a usurer brought grist to the king's
mill so did that of a prelate. However inexcusable
from a moral point of view the seizure of the issues
of vacant bishoprics and abbeys may have been, the
temptation must have been strong. For example,
the vacant abbey of Glastonbury in 1181 brought
in £600 clear, and next year the see of Lincoln accounted for £1290 and that of York for £1260 ;
Canterbury varied from £1100 to £1500. The farm
of the bishopric of Winchester in 1172 was £1555 ;
Ely produced nearly £900, and even Bath was worth
£425 clear in 1167. Very few lay honours approached
even the smallest of these sums, but with lay estates
as with clerical the death of the tenant was made a
source of profit to the king. If the heir were under
age he and his lands would be taken under the royal
protection and either managed directly for the
king's benefit or granted, for a consideration, to some
person of position, who might or might not be a relation
of the heir, while the tenant's widow could be sold
in marriage or made to pay heavily for the right of
following her own choice. Even if the heir were of
age and there were no widow to mulct, the new
tenant would have to pay " relief," or death duties,
graduated on the simple lines of getting the utmost
possible out of the landowner. For small estates
the normal rate of " relief " was £5 for a knight's
fee, the average value of a fee being at most £20,
but in the case of large estates the amount demanded
seems, as we have said, to have been arbitrarily

fixed by the king. In 1185 as much as 700 marks
was demanded of the Countess of Warwick for the
privilege of having her father's land, her dower and
liberty to remain single. To a certain extent these
enormous fines, whether inflicted as succession duties
or for other reasons, were *bruta fulmina*, defeating
their own ends. Usually the debtor contented
himself with paying yearly instalments, sometimes
round sums and sometimes strangely complicated
amounts which suggest a sudden demand from the
sheriff satisfied by a prompt clearance of pockets.
The first instalment was as a rule substantial ; Fulk
Paynel in 1180 paid 200 marks out of the 1000 marks
demanded of him for the honour of Bampton ; but
in the same year Adam de Port only paid £40 out
of a similar fine for possession of his lands and his
wife's inheritance in Normandy and for restoration
to the king's good favour. Fines might thus drag on
literally for generations, the instalments often showing a tendency to dwindle away until they ceased,
and either the king excused the payment of the rest
or the sheriff wrote it off as a bad debt. Almost any
payment on account seems to have been accepted,
and in 1187 William Fitz-Ercenbald, who owed
£2156 for arrears of farm of the silver mines of
Carlisle, paid in the rather absurd amount of
13s. 4d.

Although all these sources could be counted upon
to yield something every year the annual yield
varied greatly. There were, however, means of

raising extra occasional revenue, of which the amount
could be foretold with some accuracy. In the first
place there was the Danegeld, dating back to Saxon
times. This was a tax of two shillings on every hide
of land as rated in the Domesday Survey. It was
levied in 1156, when the accounts show that if it
had been collected in full it would have amounted
to £4550, but owing to extensive remissions and
exemptions, extending to a little over £2000, the
total yield was only £2500. For some unknown
reason this tax was only levied once more, in 1162,
and was then allowed to fall into disuse. Of more
doubtful legality but, as a rule, of greater profit
were the " aids " (auxilia, dona) assessed upon the
counties and boroughs from time to time, regulated
apparently by the king's need of money and the
taxable capacities of the districts assessed In 1156
these " aids " yielded £2100, with a further £100
still owing, while in 1159, according to Sir James
Ramsay, the amount was well over £5000. On the
latter occasion the " aids " were levied upon bishops,
certain of the wealthier lords, clerical and lay, and
Jews as well as upon the boroughs ; amongst the
biggest payments were those of the city of London
£1000, Norwich £400, York, Lincoln, and Northampton 200 marks each, the Archbishop of York
500 marks, the Bishops of Durham, Winchester, and
Lincoln a like amount, and the Abbot of St.
Augustine's, Canterbury, 220 marks. Two years
later York again paid 200 marks, but Lincoln had

risen and Norwich fallen to £200, and London escaped
with 1000 marks.

By feudal custom Henry was entitled to call for
an " aid " from his military tenants on the occasion
of his eldest daughter's marriage, and in 1168 he
availed himself of this right, stretching his demands
to include many persons outside the military classes,
to whose contributions he had no just claim. The
similar feudal " aid " for the knighting of his eldest
son was never raised, as the young king was knighted
at the time that he was in opposition to his father.
Finally, in time of war the king could call for
Scutage, a monetary composition in lieu of personal
service with the army. The amounts demanded for
Scutage varied from one to two marks for the knight's
fee, the larger sum being exactly equivalent to the
wages of a " knight," or man-at-arms, for forty
days, the period for which the tenant of a knight's
fee was bound to serve. Scutage was called for in
1156 for the war with Geoffrey of Anjou, in 1159
for the Toulouse fiasco, when £2440 is said to have
been paid, implying the commutation of the personal
service due from 1830 knights, in 1161 and 1162 for
war with France, in 1172 for the Irish expedition,
and, finally, in 1175 for the projected expedition to
Galloway. Whether the " assessment for the army
in Wales," raised in 1165, should be considered as a
scutage is questionable ; it appears to have been
more of an irregular " aid."

How far the exchequer officials of the period

indulged in anticipatory estimates of revenue, framing
their simple and elastic budgets thereon, cannot be
said. Possibly the half-yearly provisional accounts
rendered by the sheriffs at Easter enabled them to
foresee whether additional taxation would be required
to bring the revenue up to the required amount by
Michaelmas. Possibly, on the other hand, extra
taxation was put on whenever the balance in the
treasury seemed to be getting low. But however
this may have been, the annual revenue was kept by
one means or another at a pretty constant level. Sir
James Ramsay gives the totals alike for 1159, in which
year nearly £8000 were raised by scutage and " aids,"
and for 1169, when no extra taxation was levied,
as approximately £20,000. In 1176 the sum actually
paid into the treasury was £14,250, while something
like £1750 had been spent by the accountants on
the king's behalf, giving a total of £16,000. To this
have to be added the enormous sums extorted for
breach of the Forest Law. The total of the fines
inflicted on this score was £13,450, the New Forest
accounting for over £2000 and the forests of Yorkshire £1600, Bedfordshire and Buckinghamshire,
Wiltshire, Dorset and Somerset and Oxfordshire being
all above £1000. But considerably less than half the
sum demanded was paid at the time, and the total
for the year may be estimated as between £5000 and
£6000, bringing the revenue up to rather over £21,000.

The money collected by the sheriffs and other
officials was accounted for every year at Michaelmas

at the court of the exchequer. The exchequer (*scaccarium*) derived its name from the great table covered with a black chequered cloth on which the revenue accounts were set out by means of counters. It must be borne in mind that ability to read and write, though not yet considered as in itself entitling the possessor to " privilege of clergy," was so far peculiar to the clergy that a large proportion of the lay sheriffs would have been unable to keep or to understand written accounts. Even for those more learned the difficulty of working out complicated sums in Roman numerals must have been considerable, and indeed it is comparatively rare to find any lengthy medieval account in which the sums of the items correspond throughout accurately with the totals given. At the treasury courts, therefore, of England and Normandy, and possibly elsewhere, an elaboration of the " abacus," or calculating board, was introduced. This consisted of a table, ten feet long by five feet wide, covered with a black cloth on which were drawn seven vertical columns, representing, from right to left, pence, shillings, pounds, tens, hundreds, thousands, and tens of thousands of pounds. These columns in turn were divided by horizontal lines, cutting the cloth into a series of squares like those on a chess-board. Within these squares the accounts were set out with counters. At the Michaelmas session the chancellor, treasurer, and other officials, with their clerks, sat round three sides of the table, while on the other side was the calculating clerk with his counters, and near him the sheriff, who may be regarded as his opponent in the game. Along one line the calculator set out the amounts due from the accounting sheriff, and below it he gradually built up the sheriff's account, beginning with the money paid in in cash and adding item by item the sums, expended, for which the sheriff produced either the king's writs or tallies,[1] the sheriff's object being to make the two amounts balance. In this manner, by ocular demonstration, a long and complicated account could be easily followed, while for permanent record all the items were entered upon their rolls by the clerks of the chancellor and treasurer

The only coin in circulation in England at this time was the silver penny, and although sums of 12, 160, and 240 pence were spoken of as shillings, marks, and pounds for convenience of calculation, such units had no tangible existence and all money payments were made in pence. Although the money issued during Stephen's reign was poorly executed, such coins as have survived do not bear out the chroniclers' assertions that it was debased ; but it is probable that the total amount of coin in circula-

---

[1] The tally, the precursor of the counterfoil, was a wooden stick on the edge of which the sum paid was indicated by a series of cuts or notches, the various sizes of which indicated definite sums. The stick being split parallel to its face, each party to the payment retained one portion, with its edge thus significantly notched, and the genuineness of either portion could at once be proved by putting the two together, when the notches would be found to tally.

tion was small and that a considerable proportion of it was forged. In any case Henry had issued a new coinage in 1156, but the moneyers appear to have not infrequently debased the silver or made illegal profits in other ways, and in 1158 many of them had to stand their trial by the ordeal of water and several only escaped mutilation by the payment of heavy fines. Twenty years later, in 1177, we find what looks like an organised conspiracy of fraud amongst the Canterbury moneyers, five of their number being fined between them 2500 marks. At last, in 1180, Henry entrusted the reorganisation of the coinage to a foreigner, Philip Aymary, who did his work very well, but so manipulated the business to his own profit that he was banished in disgrace. This coinage, although possessing no particular artistic merit, was technically a great advance on its predecessor, and was so well appreciated that it continued to be struck, with hardly noticeable variations, under Richard and John and well into the reign of Henry III. As a result of forgery, fraud, and the inevitable loss of weight during circulation the 240 pence which constituted the nominal pound " by tale," or by number, rarely corresponded to the standard pound by weight, and as many of the sheriffs' county forms were due in " blanched " money, that is to say, in pounds of standard fineness and weight, it was necessary to test the money paid in. To begin with, pence to the value of forty-four shillings were counted out from the mass of money

SILVER PENNIES

1. First coinage of Henry II
2. Type introduced in 1180
3. Penny of Henry II struck for Aquitaine
4. Penny of Eleanor as Duchesse of Aquitaine

paid in by the sheriff whose account was under examination. Twenty shillings of this was then melted down in a crucible and purified by fire; the resulting ingot was next weighed against the standard pound, and pence added from the selected money to bring it up to weight; the number of pence required for this purpose having been noted the sheriff was charged on all " blanch " sums due that number of pence in addition to each pound by tale.

When we pass to the consideration of the relative value and purchasing power of money in the middle of the twelfth century as compared with the present time we are met by many complications. The average price of an ox or cow during this reign was from three shillings to four shillings, occasionally rising as high as five shillings ; farm horses fetched three shillings, but military chargers cost three pounds or more ; sheep ranged from fourpence to sixpence and young pigs were about the same, but when full-grown they fetched as much as a shilling. A penny a day was the recognised wage for a sergeant or private soldier, and eightpence a day for a man-at-arms ; the master of the royal yacht received a shilling, the clerk of the household two shillings, and the chancellor five shillings a day. Probably we may take the money of that date as roughly equivalent to twenty-five times the amount in modern currency.

So far as the expenditure of the Crown is concerned

o

we labour under considerable difficulties, having no
records of the nature of the Liberate and Issue Rolls
of later reigns. The only items of expenditure
which have come down to us are such as have been
entered upon the Pipe Rolls as discharged by the
sheriffs and other officers out of the issues of their
offices. The heaviest of these expenses were incurred in connection with building, and especially
in the repair and enlargement of the royal castles.
The rebuilding of Scarborough has already been
spoken of, and amongst the scores of entries of work
done on castles may be mentioned the £1000 spent
on Oxford in 1166 and 1167, a sum which is, however,
insignificant beside the £4350 spent on Dover Castle
between 1182 and 1187, as much as £1248 being
spent in the one year 1185. Nottingham, which
appears to have been one of the most habitable of
the castles, accounted for £450 in 1172 and for over
£300 in 1175 ; large sums were also spent on the
king's hunting seats such as Woodstock, Clipston,
and especially Clarendon. For the adornment of
Clarendon there were provided in 1177 " marble
columns," probably shafts of dark marble similar
to those the introduction of which by St. Hugh in
his new work at Lincoln so struck contemporary
writers. But numerous as are the entries of building
expenses, they can represent but part of the sums
laid out by Henry on such operations, nor do we
hear anything of the cost of the army or of the
upkeep of the royal household, though we know from

the existing list of salaries that this last item must have amounted to about £1500 a year. Whatever were his expenses Henry contrived to amass a great fortune, which his successor, Richard, found little difficulty in dissipating.

CHAPTER XI

SOCIETY in England during Henry's reign might be considered as arranged in three groups : (1) The Military Class, with the king at its head, ranging from the semi-independent earl to the humble tenant of some fraction of a knight's fee. (2) The Merchants and Traders—dwellers in cities and seaports, from the wealthy councillor to the humble apprentice. (3) The Peasantry—the comfortable yeoman, the farm labourer, whose theoretical lack of freedom often sat but lightly upon him, and the hired servants. From this third class the two superior classes were completed. They formed the nameless ranks of archers and foot soldiers who bore the brunt of many a battle, and, unprotected by coat of mail or prospect of ransom, paid forfeit for defeat with their lives, and they were the hardy sailors, serving the merchants in time of peace, but ever ready to convert their ships into men-of-war. It might seem that the clergy should form a fourth class, but they really fall into the same three divisions as the laity. The prelates and dignitaries, holding their lands by military service and bound to provide so many knights for the king's army, sometimes leading their troops in person; then, opposed to these sons of the Church Militant, the monks and canons of the religious orders, intent on the business of religion, not wholly averse to trading spiritual for material blessings, and displaying some skill in laying up treasure in this life as well as for the next; and finally the poor, but not always honest, parish priests and unattached clerks, the hardest workers and the worst paid, little above the secular peasantry from whose ranks they sprang, their many virtues unrecorded and the excesses of their unworthy members pilloried. If a fourth group did exist it consisted of the officials, blending the characteristics of clerks, soldiers, and merchants—men prepared at a moment's notice to hear pleas, superintend the purchase and despatch of stores, or take command of a force of soldiers.

The king's supremacy in his court was indisputable; his greatest nobles were proud to serve him, and quick to resent any infringement of their rights of service. Thus the Earl of Arundel, hereditary chief butler, returning from a long journey just as the two kings, Henry and Louis, were sitting down to dinner, strode into the hall, flung off his cloak and seized the royal goblet from the acting butler, who resisting, the powerful earl knocked him down and presented the wine on bended knee to his royal master, explaining apologetically to the French king that it was his privilege and that the deputy butler ought to have withdrawn without protest. So also, at a

later date, William de Tancarville, chamberlain of
Normandy, forcibly possessed himself of the basin
and ewer which another courtier was carrying to the
king. Yet was Henry the most accessible of men ;
out of doors he suffered his subjects to crowd round
him and speak to him freely, in his court he was
almost always ready to give informal audience to all
who sought him, and it was only at the very door
of his bedchamber that a messenger would be
challenged. Men of wit, such as Walter Map, the
cynical canon of St. Paul's, might break in on his
conversation with a humorous or sarcastic comment
unrebuked, and Henry could even take in good
part the public reprimand addressed to him by an
obscure monk of his neglected priory of Witham.
The English court under Henry attracted scholars of
European fame, and on the lighter side of literature
we find the king encouraging Gerald de Barri, the
proto-journalist, listening amusedly to his anecdotes
and bantering him, giving money to " Maurice the
story-teller " (*fabulatori*), and replying with mock
seriousness to the heroics purporting to be addressed
to him by King Arthur.

If his nobles did not share the king's literary tastes
they were at least in tune with him on the subject
of sport. Hunting and hawking were the recreations
of the English and Norman nobility, and in his de-
votion thereto Henry yielded to none of his subjects.
The keepers of his hounds formed not the most insignificant part of his retinue ; hawks were procured

for him from Norway and from Ireland and passed
as presents between himself and foreign princes ;
when he went out of England, whether for peaceful
cause or war, his hawks and hounds and huntsmen
followed him. His sons also, like all the magnates
of their days, were devotees of the chase, but the
two elder found greater pleasure in the sport of war,
and the young King Henry in particular shone as
the patron of the tournament. The gradual re-
pression of private warfare, at least between the
smaller lords, had deprived life of much of its excitement, and the more warlike spirits sought to
counteract what they no doubt considered the
softness and degeneracy of the age by the institution
of tournaments, a species of private war cleansed
of personal rancour and lacking the disastrous consequences to lands and tenants involved by the real
thing. To picture the tournament of this date as
resembling the formal and chivalrous jousting in the
lists of later centuries would be completely misleading. For the most part the frequenters of these
meetings were landless men, younger sons and needy
adventurers, intent solely, or at least mainly, on
making money by the capture of opponents, whose
chargers and armour then became their own, and
whose bodies might be held to ransom. It was no
shame for ten to set on one, and William the Marshal,
one of the most brilliant of these adventurers and
the instructor of the young king, gained praise by
the skill with which he let his adversaries exhaust

themselves before he flung his forces upon them.   This
same Marshal, who went with another knight on a
pot-hunting expedition during which they accounted
for 103 knights, besides extra chargers, on one
occasion saw one of the opposing knights thrown by
his horse and lying on the ground, disabled with a
broken thigh ; rushing out of the tent where he was
dining he picked up the injured man and bore him
back into the tent, handing him over a prisoner to
his companions "to pay their debts with."   In this
particular instance there was no doubt an element of
rough humour, but the whole spirit of the tournament
was practical and unromantic, though fame and
glory were sought at the same time as wealth, and
the Marshal would have set a higher value upon
his reputation for skill and courage than upon the
fund of ready money for which he was remarkable
at a time when steel and silver were rarely found
together.

   The spirit of the tournament pervaded the field
of battle, and so far as the knightly combatants were
concerned their chief aim was to capture and hold
to ransom their adversaries rather than to kill them.
Such lust of slaughter as they felt was satisfied at
the expense of the unfortunate infantry, drawn from
the ranks of the peasants and yeomen and not worth
ransoming.   After a desperate and decisive battle
the chroniclers will recount a long list of knights
captured, but it is rare indeed that any are recorded
to have fallen in battle, and on such rare occasions

it was usually by the hand of a common foot soldier or by a chance arrow. It was precisely this tradition of the respect due to gentle blood that made the Norman knights so useless against the Welsh or Irish, who ignored their gentility and fought to kill.

Henry's genius for organisation found scope in military matters as elsewhere. During the reigns of the Saxon kings the *fyrd* or national militia, theoretically consisting of all the able-bodied male population, was always liable to be called out in time of war, and this liability had remained in force after the Conquest. Under William the Conqueror the country had been parcelled out into estates, great and small, the tenants of which held by the service of supplying a fixed quota of knights, in no way proportionate to the size or value of the estate, to serve in the royal army for forty days when required. It has been already pointed out that Henry II. encouraged the system of commuting personal service for a money payment, and in order to ascertain the exact amount of service due he caused a general return to be made by his military tenants in 1166. They were required to state how many knights they were bound to find, and as there were two ways of providing for these knights, either by granting them land in return for their services when required or by hiring them as occasion demanded, a distinction was to be drawn between the knights enfeoffed and those chargeable on the demesnes. A further distinction was to be made between those knights already enfeoffed at the time of the death of Henry I. and those of newer feoffment. In many cases the greater barons had enfeoffed more knights than they were bound to supply, probably for the most part during Stephen's reign, with the intention of augmenting their own private forces, and Henry claimed that they should pay scutage on this larger number of knights instead of on their original quota, a claim which was strenuously resisted.

For the re-organisation of the national forces an Assize of Arms was issued in England in 1181. Every holder of a knight's fee or of rents and property to the value of sixteen marks was to keep a coat of mail, a helmet, a shield, and a lance ; the owner of property worth ten marks should have a hauberk, an iron headpiece, and a lance, and all burgesses and the whole body of freemen should have a quilted jacket (*wambais*), an iron headpiece, and a lance. These arms were never to be parted with, but to descend from father to son; but in order to render the supply more accessible it was ordered that no burgess should keep more arms than his statutory quota, and if he had others should give or sell them to those that required them ; at the same time Jews were forbidden to retain coats of mail and hauberks, presumably the most expensive portions of the outfit. From the absence of any mention of horses it has been assumed by some writers that all these troops were expected to fight on foot, but this is undoubtedly an error; presumably the provision of a horse was left to the discretion of the soldier, and practically the whole of the first class and a large proportion of the second would have been mounted men. Another noteworthy omission is that of the bow ; some thirty years later the holder of property worth twenty shillings was required to provide a bow and arrows, but at this time it would seem that the bow was regarded as unworthy of a freeman and its use confined to the villein soldiers.

The justices itinerant were to publish this assize in the different county courts and to make it known that any defaulter would pay for his fault with his body and by no means escape with fine or forfeiture. At the same time the justices were to hold inquiries by juries of freemen of good standing as to the persons in the several hundreds and boroughs who held property worth sixteen marks or ten marks, to draw up lists of such persons and to swear them to the observance of the assize.

The final article of the Assize of Arms directed that no one should buy or sell any ship to be taken away from England, or export timber. In this decree we have evidence of Henry's comprehension of the value of a strong navy to the country. In speaking of a strong navy it must not be supposed that any royal force of fighting ships existed or was even contemplated at this time. Such naval organisation as existed was almost entirely confined to the federation of the Cinque Ports. The origin and early history of this federation is very obscure, but it seems clear that Hastings and Dover and probably the other three ports of Sandwich, Hythe, and Romney, were bound together by the possession of common privileges and common responsibilities in the reign of Edward the Confessor. Hastings was the undoubted head of this group of ports and the first to acquire privileges at the royal court and in connection with the herring fishery at Yarmouth which were afterwards extended to the other members. When the title of the Cinque Ports was assumed has not yet been discovered, but it was clearly established by the beginning of the reign of Henry II., as in 1161 we find a payment of £34, 17s. to the ships of " the five ports " which conveyed treasure across the channel. As one main division of the English fleet employed in the expedition against Lisbon in 1147 was referred to as the " Hastingenses," almost certainly alluding to the ships of the allied ports, it would seem that the title was first officially recognised under Henry II. The bonds of union were still so loose that the separate ports and their affiliated members received separate charters. One of these, of quite uncertain date, issued by Henry at Westminster, confirmed to the " barons " of Hastings their privileges at court, exemption from customs and other dues, and the foreshore rights of " strand and den " at Yarmouth, in return for the provision of twenty ships for fifteen days when required. Henry also granted similar

exemptions to the two " ancient towns " of Rye
and Winchelsea, affiliating them to Hastings, to
whose quota of twenty ships they were to send two ;
they were further exempted from the jurisdiction
of the ordinary courts and might be impleaded only
in the same manner as the barons of Hastings and
of the Cinque Ports. This privilege of a separate
court was clearly of early date, as in another charter
given during the first six years of Henry's reign to
the men of Hythe he ordered that they should not
plead elsewhere than they were used to do, namely
at the Shipway.

As a result of grants and confirmations of privileges
the king could rely at need upon a force of some sixty
ships. The ships themselves were the ordinary
fishing and trading vessels of the channel ports,
small but seaworthy, easily converted into fighting
ships by the erection of wooden fore and stern castles
and manned by hardy and experienced sailors. But
for all their experience the little ships with their
single square sail were not very manageable in a
storm and the tale of shipwrecks was large. When
used for transport purposes it would seem that about
a hundred soldiers could be carried by each vessel.
The Cinque Port vessels were bound to carry a crew
of twenty-one, but this was apparently an exceptional complement, as in the levy of ships for the
Irish expedition of 1171 the average crew was twelve
men and a master, such crews being carried by the
thirty-six ships from Norfolk and Suffolk, the seven

from Dorset and Somerset, six from Devon, two
from London, and one from Herefordshire; on the
other hand the twenty-eight ships supplied by
Gloucestershire averaged only six men, but eight
from Sussex nineteen, and two from Hampshire
twenty-two apiece. During the troubles of 1173
most of the ships which were "sent to Sandwich to
meet the ships of the Cinque Ports" carried crews
of twenty or upwards, and the two vessels from
Colchester carried sixty seamen between them. Probably the numbers were raised at this time in anti-
cipation of attack, as we find that an extra force of
from ten to twenty men was put on board the king's
yacht each time it crossed with treasure this year.
This royal yacht was the only vessel permanently
retained in the king's service, naval forces being
collected as required from the Cinque Ports and other
coast towns, though there were at Southampton
certain private ship-owners whose vessels were so
often chartered for national service that they might
almost be held to have constituted a miniature royal
navy in embryo.

Southampton was at this time the chief mercantile
port of England, pre-eminent for its valuable wine
trade, thanks alike to the natural advantages of its
situation relative to Normandy and the wine-ex-
porting districts of the west, and to its proximity
to the royal city of Winchester. Although London
had already outdistanced Winchester in wealth the
latter was still the home of the treasury, the rival of

Westminster as the king's official residence, and a leading centre of trade. The great fair of St. Giles drew merchants from all over England and from foreign lands to Winchester, to sell their fine worked stuffs to the king's purveyors for his royal robes or to buy the coarse woollen cloth of local manufactures, for Winchester with its gilds of weavers and fullers was a great seat of the cloth industry, most of its products being the coarse " burrell " cloth of which two thousand ells were purchased and sent to Ireland in 1171 for the troops. A cheaper and coarser cloth seems to have been made in Cornwall, as on several occasions Cornish " burrells " in large quantities were bought for the king's almoner. The output of English cloth was altogether more remarkable for quantity than quality ; gilds of weavers existed in 1156 at Winchester, London, Lincoln, Oxford, Huntingdon, and Nottingham, all being of sufficient importance to pay yearly to the king from 40s. to £6, but their productions were for the most part poor and coarse, with the notable exception of the scarlet cloths of Lincoln, which are found fetching the prodigious price of 6s. 8d. the ell. So far as there were exceptions to the general lack of quality they were no doubt due to foreign, especially to Flemish, influence. At the time of the expulsion of the Flemings after the rebellion of 1173 there are numerous entries on the Pipe Rolls recording seizures of wool and woad belonging to Flemings; the dyers of Worcester are recorded as owing £12

to the king's Flemish enemies, and there is other
evidence to show the presence of these skilled clothworkers throughout the country.

For foreign trade, statistics, and even such details
as would permit of broad generalisations, are lacking. There was no imposition of customs for revenue
purposes by the central authorities; each town,
whether seaport or inland market, had its own
schedule of customs and *octroi* dues, but they were
only under the control of the Crown in so far that
the king could by charter exempt persons from
the payment of such dues throughout the realm.
Such exemptions were amongst the most valued
franchises of the barons of the Cinque Ports, the
men of a few privileged boroughs, and the tenants
of certain great religious houses. A trading privilege
of particular interest for its bearing upon the development of London under Norman influence was
the right of the citizens of Rouen to a port or anchor-
age in the Thames close to the city walls, which
was confirmed to them by Henry II. in 1174. A
still more striking instance of the connection of
two ports was Henry's grant of Dublin to the burgesses of Bristol, assuring to them a virtual monopoly of the Irish trade, which they appear to have
previously shared with Chester, the monopoly of
the Irish trade with Normandy being in the same
way assured to Rouen. As a whole Henry's policy
towards the towns and trading communities, especially in the earlier years of his reign, was liberal

and encouraging ; we find him granting the customs of York to the burgesses of Scarborough in 1155, the liberties of London and Winchester to the men of Gloucester, and the customs of Lincoln to the burgesses of Coventry at a later date ; gilds merchant and trade gilds were confirmed in their privileges at Oxford, Nottingham, Lincoln, and elsewhere, and the formation of others licensed. With the growth of trade other unauthorised gilds sprang up, and in 1180 no fewer than nineteen such " adulterine " gilds were reported in London alone, five of them being connected with London Bridge, the famous stone bridge built in 1176. Of these London gilds the only four definitely identified with special trades were those of the goldsmiths, spicers, butchers, and clothworkers, the others being, no doubt, social and religious societies of a less specialised composition.

Side by side with the growth of manufactures developed the exploitation of the mineral wealth of England. The lead mines of Derbyshire, Yorkshire, and Shropshire were being worked, and the valuable silver-bearing lead mines of Carlisle, which were farmed in 1158 for 100 marks, were bringing in 150 marks at the end of the reign, having fluctuated between 500 marks in 1166 and no yield at all after the border wars of 1173–4. At the other end of the kingdom were the rich tin mines of Cornwall and Devon. Iron was worked in the northern counties and to some extent in Northamptonshire,

P

but the industry had not yet attained any degree
of importance in the Weald of Sussex and Kent,
and the Forest of Dean enjoyed a practical
monopoly of the southern iron trade. Tin was
undoubtedly exported to the Continent, lead we
read of as sent by King Henry for the use of the
monks of Clairvaux; but it is doubtful whether it
was to any extent an article of commerce, and iron
was almost certainly not exported.

By a curious inversion of later practice the chief
exports from England in early times were the raw
materials of wool and hides and a certain amount
of food stuffs. Amongst the latter were no doubt
cheeses, which had already found a market in Flanders
in the eleventh century, and possibly ale, for which
England, and especially Kent, was celebrated. In
1168 we find fifty-three hogsheads of ale sent to
the king in Normandy, and that this drink was
appreciated by foreigners we may conclude from its
having occupied so prominent a part amongst the gifts
which Becket carried with him on his famous embassy
to the French court. While ale was the national
drink, no small quantity of wine was grown in
England, vineyards existing in the southern counties
from Kent to Hereford, and at least as far north as
Cambridgeshire, and references to cider are also
numerous.

The preference given to cider over Kentish ale
was one of the charges of luxury brought by Gerald
de Barri against his monastic entertainers at the

cathedral priory of Christchurch, Canterbury. How far the accusations of excess, in food and in other matters, brought by Gerald and by Walter Map against the monks, and in particular against those of the Cistercian order, could be sustained is a question difficult to answer. Both men bore personal grudges against the Cistercians, both preferred a scandalous story or a witty jest to strict accuracy, and Gerald especially was utterly unscrupulous in the abuse of his enemies. At the same time some of the little details in the stories told seem to support their accuracy, and there is evidence that in many cases abuses had crept in and ascetic ideals been relaxed with a rapidity which is astonishing when it is remembered that Bernard of Clairvaux, the founder of the order, had died only the year before Henry ascended the throne. One of Gerald's tales relates how an abbot of one of the English Cistercian houses hospitably regaled the king, not knowing him, with a drinking bout, initiating him into the mysteries of " Pril " and " Vril," the private toasts, or drinking cries, used in the monastery in place of the secular " Washeil " and " Drinkheil," and how Henry, when the abbot subsequently came to court, welcomed him with " Pril " and made him repeat the performance, to his utter confusion and the intense amusement of the nobles. The possibility of this being a true story is increased when we read in the Cistercian annals a generation later that in 1215 the Abbot of Beaulieu was deposed because he behaved outrageously at table, drinking hilariously, in the presence of three earls and forty knights, and that, two years later, the Abbot of Tintern drank ceremoniously (*solemniter*) with bishops and monks. Of the purely English order of Gilbertines, whose founder, Gilbert of Sempringham, died in 1181, Gerald speaks favourably, though deprecating their system of double convents for nuns and canons, but it is only of the austere Carthusians and Grammontanes that he writes with whole-hearted commendation. That his praise was justified is confirmed by the exceptional favour shown to these two orders by Henry, who troubled little about other religious, save the nuns of Fontevrault and the military order of the Templars.

Gluttony and drunkenness were indeed vices in their addiction to which the English, both clergy and laity, compared unfavourably with their Welsh and Irish contemporaries. William Fitz-Stephen, in his famous description of London, gives " the immoderate drinking of fools " as one of the two " plagues " of the city. The degree of luxury then prevalent at table is indicated by his account of the public cook-shop on the river bank near the wine wharves, where every variety of fish, flesh, and fowl, roast meat, baked meat, stew and pasty was ever preparing. Hither ran the servants of those upon whose empty larders unexpected guests had descended ; here was store sufficient to satisfy an army of knights or a band of pilgrims ; here an epicure might call for sturgeon, woodcock, or ortolan. It was a gay, busy, prosperous city, ships of all nations loading and unloading, crowds chaffering with the merchants and tradesmen, whose stalls were congregated according to kind; here the booths of the goldsmiths, and here a street of cloth merchants; here the grocers, and here a row of cutlers, while through the narrow, irregular streets, scattering purchasers and loafers, would pass the retinue of some prelate or baron on the way to his town house. Then there was the weekly excitement of the horse fair held outside the city walls on the flat fields of Smithfield; every one was there, come to buy, to sell, or to look on, and there were horses to suit every conceivable want, at least if you accepted the word of their owners; here were ambling nags, unbroken colts, of whose heels you had better be careful, stately chargers, sturdy pack horses, mares with their foals, cart horses, driving horses, horses innumerable. But the fun really began when, with a sudden shouting, the crowd parted hastily and left a clear course down which thundered the chargers in mad race, scarcely needing the shouts and spurring of their boy jockeys to urge them to their utmost effort. And then there were the holidays, when the fields outside the city were thronged with students, chaffing each other and lampooning their teachers with apt Latinity, young nobles from the court at Westminster, and apprentices from the city, while their elders looked on and

grew younger with excitement as they watched
them cock-fighting, ball-playing, or tilting; and
as the day wore on the girls would come to the
fore and there would be song and dancing until
the moon rose. Or the scene would shift to the
river, where the boys, standing in the bows of a
boat, would tilt at a shield suspended above the
water and win either the applause or more often
the laughter of the watchers on the bridge and in the
riverside houses by their efforts to maintain their
balance and avoid a ducking. And then in the
winter, when the marshes were covered with ice,
bone skates were in demand, and tilting on skates
warmed the blood even if it was responsible for
rather a large number of broken heads and limbs.
For those who were too old, too timid, or too dignified for such boisterous sports there were the
pleasures of hunting and hawking over the great
preserves belonging to the city in Hertfordshire,
Middlesex, and Kent. A gay city, but one whose
gaiety was only too often suddenly checked by an
outbreak of fire, the second of Fitz-Stephen's
" plagues." With their wooden hovels, wooden
booths, and primitive open hearths the English
towns were constant sufferers from fire. Becket's
parents had been impoverished by a succession of
fires, and in one year, 1161, London, Canterbury,
Winchester, and Exeter were devastated; next
year the booths of St. Giles' fair at Winchester were
burnt with all the merchandise in them, and in

1180 a fire beginning at the mint destroyed the greater part of the unfortunate town of Winchester; Glastonbury was burnt in 1184 and Chichester in 1187; and these are only instances recorded for the magnitude of destruction wrought; smaller outbreaks must have been of continual occurrence.

The description of London, *mutatis mutandis*, would apply sufficiently well to other towns of the period, though in many of the smaller boroughs the mercantile element must be almost eliminated and a large agricultural element introduced to render the picture even tolerably faithful. But when we get outside the walls of the towns we meet with quite a different state of affairs. Here and there a castle or the chief seat of some powerful landowner would present us with a building of some architectural importance, but in far the greater number of cases the chief house, the manor, would be a barn-like structure of one storey, the main feature of which would be the hall, or living room, with the massive beams of its open roof blackened by the smoke from the fire burning on an open hearth in the centre of the hall. The chamber, or sleeping apartment, a similar but smaller room connected with the first by a lobby or vestibule, would possibly be partitioned into cubicles either by lath and plaster walls or by cloth hangings. The kitchen, with brew-house, wash-house, dairy and other offices, where such existed, might form part of the main buildings or be in a block by themselves,

and there would be one or two barns, with cart-
houses, stables, cow-sheds, hen-houses, pig-styes and
the miscellaneous appurtenances of a farm.   The
roofs of the various buildings would be thatched
and the windows unglazed, closed with wooden
shutters ; on the floor would be a layer of rushes,
not too frequently renewed, and one or two trestle
tables, some benches and stools; a cupboard and
possibly a couple of massive chests would pretty
nearly exhaust the catalogue of the furniture, save
for the wooden platters and bowls, buckets and
barrels in the kitchen. Near the manor house as
a rule would stand the church, massive and dark,
its walls adorned with crudely realistic paintings
and its stonework enriched with the strong, barbaric mouldings of the period, and hard by, over-
shadowed by the tithe barn, would be the house of
the parish priest, little superior to the clusters of
mud huts in which the peasantry contrived to
exist.

To obtain a true estimate of the position of the
peasantry at this time it is essential to grasp the
entirely different standard of life then prevalent.
Comfort and happiness are mainly matters of comparison, and at a time when the country gentleman
was content with a simplicity which a modern
artisan would scorn the labourer might well see no
discomfort in conditions against which an Irish
peasant would protest   A condition of servitude
was no great burden in itself to those upon

whose imaginations the theoretical beauty of liberty had not dawned. The gradations between free and bond were so fine that it required a skilled lawyer to draw the line that separated them, and in practice many freemen were worse off than the average villein. If villeinage legally bound the tenant to perform irksome service for his lord it morally bound the lord to provide for his tenant. At the same time the services exacted from the villein were arduous; in theory they were unlimited, but in practice custom had already fixed their nature in most manors. Striking a rough average, we may say that a villein as a rule had to work for his lord one day in each week for every five or ten acres that he held, and in addition to put in a number of extra days during the busy and critical weeks of harvest and further occasional days for plough-ing, harrowing, and sowing. Then there were occa-sions when he might be called upon to help in thatch-ing the farm buildings, carting manure, repairing hedges, carrying farm produce to market or fetching salt, or such local requirements as the drying and salting of herrings. For many of these extra ser-vices he had some return in the shape of a meal at the lord's cost, but the demands upon his time were heavy and would have left him little opportunity to cultivate his own small holding if he had no sons or others to assist him.

The lot of the people, villein, landowner, and burgess had improved under the wise rule of Henry, and even the great lords, if shorn of their power, were safe from the attacks of rivals and secure of their possessions so long as they remained loyal. The seeds of the English Constitution had been sown. The English nation, which had been nursed, in part unwittingly, by Henry, was to discover its own existence under his successors when his foreign policy failed and the connection between Normandy and England was severed. The relations between Church and State were settled upon a firm basis, and if the supremacy of the State, for which Henry had fought, had to be abandoned, the Catholic Church in England developed a consciousness of nationality and remained independent of Rome in a degree quite exceptional when compared with the Church on the Continent. As the effects of Henry's policy were either evanescent and negligible or enduring, and in the latter case easy to trace, it is not hard to estimate the significance of his reign, but to obtain a just estimate of the man himself is more difficult. For the more intimate details we are largely dependent upon men who either bore him ill-will or, more rarely, were writing in a spirit of flattery, but putting the evidence together we see a strong, clear-headed man, controlling his emotions but occasionally clearing off accumulations of irritation and annoyance by tremendous outbursts of mad rage ; a methodical man with a keen sense of justice, but arbitrary and unscrupulous ; a skilled general who never engaged in warfare

if it could be avoided ; a keen and restless sportsman with a sense of humour and a passion for
literature ; a free-thinking adulterer with a genuine
appreciation of purity and true religion ; a king who
could manage the affairs of half-a-dozen principali-
ties but could not rule his own house ; an acute
judge of men, who lavished affection and benefits
upon ungrateful and unworthy sons ; a mass of
contradictions ; in other words, an entirely human
man.

BIBLIOGRAPHY

RECORDS

FOR the whole period covered by the reign of Henry II. the English national archives are fortunate in the possession of the unique series of Pipe Rolls. On these annual account rolls were entered in detail the issues of all the counties, escheats, vacant sees and other lands farmed for the Crown. The details of these payments, including "relief" paid by the heirs of deceased tenants in chief, amercements for innumerable offences and other miscellaneous information, are most valuable to the genealogist, topographer, and constitutional historian, but of greater value to the general historian are the balancing items of money expended by the sheriffs upon building operations, hiring ships, provisioning troops, entertaining members of the royal family or ambassadors from foreign courts, and in a hundred other different ways. From these it is possible in many cases to follow the king's movements, while often the details given throw a cold, impartial light, corroborative or corrective, upon the prejudiced or distorted statements of the chroniclers. Of the corresponding Pipe Rolls for Normandy only that for 1180 and a fragment for 1185 have survived.

A large number of royal *Charters* of this period have survived and are of great value to the antiquary, though, for the most part, they yield little to the general historian. The *Calendars of Charter Rolls,* Mr. Round's *Calendar of Documents preserved in France,* and the *Monasticon Anglicanum* contain the most important collections of these charters. With practically no exceptions the charters of Henry II. are undated and can only be assigned to their years by a careful examination of the attesting signatures, but M. Leopold Delisle in a series of articles in the *Bibliothèque de l'École des Chartes* (1906–1908) claims that the charters prior to 1173 can be at once distinguished from those of later date by the absence from the king's title of the formula *Dei gratia*, which is invariably found from 1173 onwards. This theory has been disputed, but the weight of evidence is in favour of M. Delisle.

Surveys of the manors and churches belonging to the canons of St. Paul's, made in 1181 (printed in the *Domesday of St. Paul's* by the Camden Society), and of the possessions of the Knights Templars in 1185 (Exch. K. R., Misc. Books, vol. 16) are of interest for the light thrown upon land tenure and agricultural life in general, and further particulars can be gleaned from the many monastic cartularies, printed and manuscript, which exist. Most important, perhaps, of all this class of records is the "Boldon Book," an elaborate survey of the possessions of the see of Durham in 1183, which has been fully treated by Dr. Lapsley in the *Victoria History of the County of Durham.*

The *Red Book of the Exchequer*, which has been printed in the Rolls Series, contains the important returns of knights' fees made in 1166 and the "Constitutio Domus Regis," an account of persons composing the king's household, their wages and perquisites, originally compiled in the reign of Henry I., but equally applicable to the court of Henry II.

CHRONICLES

For the acts of Henry prior to his accession we are mainly dependent upon the concise records of the *Anglo-Saxon Chronicle* and Henry of Huntingdon, with the valuable addition of the more detailed *Gesta Stephani.*

For the general history of the reign the *Chronicles* of Robert of Torigny, Abbot of Mont St. Michel, down to 1186, in which year he died, and the *History* of William of Newburgh are two of the most reliable sources. From 1170 onwards we have the valuable aid of the *Gesta Henrici,* known by the name of Abbot Benedict of Peterborough, which is incorporated in the *Chronicles* of Roger of Hoveden. The works of Ralph de Diceto, Dean of St. Paul's, and of Gervase of Canterbury are for the most part compilations based upon other writers, but each contain a few facts not found elsewhere. The *Annales Monastici* and other monastic chronicles printed in the Rolls Series and the *Annales Angevines (Collection de Textes)* supply a few occasional details of local events and serve to corroborate the more important works.

The bulk of the literature concerned with the Becket controversy has been collected in the seven volumes of Canon J. C. Robertson's *Materials for the History of Thomas Becket* in the Rolls Series. These contain the *Lives* by William of Canterbury, including a long list of Miracles, Benedict of Peterborough, John of Salisbury, continued by Alan of Tewkesbury, William Fitz-Stephen, Herbert of Bosham, Edward Grim and two anonymous biographers, and also over eight hundred *Letters* connected with the controversy. Some light is thrown on the contemporary estimate of Becket by the Latin metrical chronicle, *Draco Normannicus,* attributed to Etienne of Rouen and written before Becket's martyrdom had conferred upon him exemption from criticism.

Welsh affairs are recorded in the *Annales Cambriæ* and the more detailed *Brut y Tynysogion,* and much light is thrown upon them by the *Descriptio Cambriæ* and the *Itinerarium Cambriæ* of Gerald de Barri (" Giraldus Cambrensis "). The same writer's *Topographia Hibernica* gives an interesting but inaccurate account of Ireland, and his *Expugnatio Hiberniæ* recounts the conquest of Ireland by Richard " Strongbow," Earl of Pembroke, and his companions. Another and more reliable account of the conquest is given in the Norman poem, *The Song of Dermot and the Earl* (ed. G. H. Orpen, 1891); it appears to have been based upon materials supplied by Morice Regan, secretary to King Dermot. In addition to these sources we have, for Irish history, the *Annals of the Four Masters* and the *Annals of Loch Cé*.

Jordan Fantosme has left us a spirited Norman poem on the war between England and Scotland in 1173–4, including the capture of the Scottish king, at which he was present. Another poem, *Guillaume le Maréchal* (ed. P. Meyer, Société de l'Histoire de France), throws considerable light upon Henry's later years, as does the *De Principis Instructione* of Gerald de Barri and the *Vita Hugonis*, or Life of St. Hugh of Lincoln.

On the legal and constitutional side we have Glanville *De Legibus*, a formulary compiled by the justiciar about the end of Henry's reign, and the *Dialogus de Scaccario* of Richard Fitz-Neal, an elaborate account, historical and technical, of the exchequer.

In the matter of illustrating the life of the times first place must be accorded to Gerald de Barri, who exhibits in a unique degree the qualifications of a journalist; clever, humorous, plucky, possessing immense self-confidence, a fund of quotations, a love of "purple patches" and an eloquence of abuse worthy of his Welsh extraction, he continually enlivens his pages with personal anecdotes, usually scandalous. With him may be classed Walter Map, Archdeacon of Oxford, witty and sarcastic. The *Maréchal* poem, already mentioned, throws some light on the life of the nobles, more especially of the younger landless men, whose chief delight was in the tournament. The inner life of a monastery is shown with singular fidelity in the *Chronicle* of Jocelin of Brakelond, monk of Bury St. Edmunds, and a few details of the general life of the people may be gleaned from the writings of Alexander Neckam.

MODERN WRITERS

The reign of Henry II. has been treated by Lord Lyttleton, and more recently by Miss Norgate and by Mrs. J. R. Green. The period is also covered by the third volume of Sir J. Ramsay's solid and scholarly *History of England*. Mr. Eyton in his *Household and Itinerary of Henry II.* endeavoured to trace the movements of the restless king from day to day and to assign to definite occasions his undated charters. Complete success in such a task is not to be expected, but although there are a number of mistakes, especially in the dating of charters, the work is monumental and most valuable to the student. Finally, mention may be made of Mr. Round's various papers in *Geoffrey de Mandeville, Feudal England,* and *The Commune of London*.

APPENDIX

ITINERARY OF HENRY II

Tⁱⁱⁱˢ itinerary is based upon Eyton's monumental work, the sources being, first, the definite statements of the chroniclers; secondly, the evidence of records, more particularly the Pipe Rolls, which prove the presence of the king at certain places in the course of the year but do not as a rule give an exact date; and thirdly, royal charters, which can be dated within certain limits by the names of the witnesses. Where the name of a place is given with a date in brackets, it indicates that the place was visited during the year under which it appears, but that the exact date is problematic. In cases where charters given at a particular place can be assigned with reasonable probability, but not with certainty, to a particular year, the place name is put in brackets.

1154		1155	
December 7 .	. Barfleur	January 13 .	. Oxford
„ 8 .	. Coast of Hamp-	[January,	[Northampton]
	shire (Henry	February,	York
	lands)	March]	Scarborough
	Winchester		[Lincoln]
„ 19 .	. Westminster		[Peterborough]
	(coronation)		[Thorney]
„ 25 .	. Bermondsey		[Ramsey]
			Nottingham

241

Q

1155 (*continued*)

March [c. 27]	London
April 10 . . .	. Wallingford
[May, June].	. Cleobury
	Wigmore
	Bridgnorth
July 7 . . .	. Bridgnorth
[July, August,	[Worcester]
September]	[Salisbury]
September 20	. Winchester
[October,	Cricklade
November,	Woodstock
December]	Windsor
December 25	. Westminster

1156

January 2–10	Dover
„ [11–31]	Wissant
	[St Omer]
February 2 .	. Rouen
„ 5 .	. near Gisors
[February–	Anjou
August]	Mirebeau, in
	Poitou
	Chinon, in
	Touraine
	Loudun, in
	Touraine
[September 1]	Saumur
[October]	Limoges
December 25	. Bordeaux

1157

[January–	Normandy
March]	
April [c. 8] .	. Barfleur
	Southampton
	London

[May] . . .	. Ongar
May 19 . .	. Bury St.
	Edmunds
„ 23–28 .	. Colchester
[June]. . .	. [Thetford]
	[Norwich]
July 17 . .	. Northampton
[July] . . .	. The Peak
	Chester
[August] . .	. North Wales
December 13	. Gloucester
„ 25	. Lincoln

1158

[January]	. . Carlisle
[February,	[Blythe]
March]	[Nottingham]
	The Peak
April 20 . .	. Worcester
[April–August].	[Evesham]
	[Tewkesbury]
	Gloucester
	Wells
	Cheddar
	Brill
	Clarendon
	[Westminster]
	Brockenhurst
	Winchester
August 14 .	. Portsmouth
	(Henry
	crosses to
	Normandy)
[August] . .	. near Gisors
September 8 .	. Argentan
[September] .	. Paris
September 29	. Avranches
October [c. 9]	. Nantes
[October]. .	. Thouars

[November] . . Le Mans
November 23 . Mont St.
    Michael
[November, Avranches
December] Bayeux
    Caen
    Rouen
December 25 . Cherbourg

1159

[? April] . . . Blaye in
    Guienne
    Poitiers
May 21–23 . . Bec Hellouin
  „ 24 . . . Rouen
June 6–8 . . . Hilliricourt
  „ 24 . . . Poitiers
  „ 30 . . . Perigueux
July 1–3 . . . Agen
  „ [c. 5] . . Auvillards
July–Septem- Toulouse
ber [c. 26]
[October] . . . Uzerche
    Limoges
    Beauvais
[November] . . Guerberoi
    Estrepagny
December 25 . Falaise

1160

    Normandy
July . . . . Neufmarché
November 2 . . Neufbourg
December 25 . Le Mans

1161

    Normandy
March 1 . . Mortimer-en-
    Lions

[March] . . . [Lions-la-
    Forêt]
    Le Mans
[May, June] . . The Vexin
    near Chateau-
    dun
July–August . Châtillon (? on
  10 the Garonne)
[October] . . . Fréteval
December 25 . Bayeux

1162

February 25 . Rouen
[March] . . . Lillebone
    Fécamp
[April] . . . Rouen
[May] . . . . Falaise
    Normandy
[September] . . Choisi on the
    Loire
[December] . . Barfleur
December 25 . Cherbourg

1163

January 25 . . Southampton
[February] . . Oxford
    Salisbury
March 3–6 . . London
  „ 8 . . . Westminster
  „ 17 . . . Canterbury
  „ 19 . . . Dover
  „ 31 . . . Windsor
April . . . . Reading
    Wallingford
[May] . . . . Wales
[June] . . . . Carlisle
    York
    Northampton

1163 (continued)

July 1 . . . . Woodstock
[July, August] . London
              Windsor
October 1, 2 . . Westminster
[October–   Northampton
  December   Lincoln
            The Peak
            Gloucester
            Oxford
December 25 . Berkhamp-
              stead

1164

January 13–28 . Clarendon
[March] . . . Porchester
            Woodstock
April 12 . . . London
  „ 19 . . . Reading
c. August 24– Woodstock
c. September 10
September 14 . Westminster
October 6–20 . Northampton
December 24–26 Marlborough

1165

[February] . . [Westminster]
[March] . . . Normandy
April 11 . . . Gisors
  „ [15] . . Rouen
May . . . . Southampton
           Surrey
           Rhuddlan
           Basingwerk
[July] . . . . Shrewsbury
           Oswestry
[August] . . . Powys
           Chester

[September–   Westminster
  December]   Woodstock
December 25 . Oxford

1166

February . . . Clarendon
March [c. 20] . Southampton
[April] . . . Maine
           Alençon
           Roche-Mabille
April 24 . . . Angers
May 10–17 . . Le Mans
June 1 . . . Chinon
  „ 28 . . . near Fougères
July 12–14 . . Fougères
[August,   Rennes
  September] Rédon
           Combour
           Dol
           Mont St Michel
           Thouars
[October,   Caen
  November] Touques
           Rouen
           Caen
November 18 . Tours
  „ 20 . Chinon
December 25 . Poitiers

1167

January . . . Guienne
February, March Gascony
April . . . . Auvergne
May . . . . Normandy
June 4 . . . The Vexin
[July] . . . . Chaumont
[August] . . . The Vexin
           Rouen

APPENDIX

245

September . . Brittany
October . . . [Valognes]
Caen
November 26–
December 4 . Argentan
[December] . . Le Mans
December 25 . Argentan

1168

January . . . Poitou
[March] . . . Normandy
April 7 . . . Pacey
May . . . . Brittany
Vannes
Porhoet
Cornouaille
June . . . . Dinan
St. Malo
Heddé
„ 24 . . . Bécherell
Tinténiac
„ 25 . . . Leon
[July] . . . . La Ferté Bernard
[August   Ponthieu
September] Brueroles
Neufchâtel
Norman frontier
[October] . . . Perche
December 25–31 Argentan

1169

January 1 . . Argentan
„ 6 . . Montmirail
March . . . . St. Germain-en-Laye
Poitou

[April] . . . St. Machaire
May–July . . Gascony
August . . . Angers
„ 15 . . Argentan
„ 23, 24 . Damfront
„ 31 . . Bayeux
September 1, 2 . Bur-le-Roi
„ 3–
October . . Rouen
November 16 . St. Denis
„ 18 . Montmartre
December 25 . Nantes

1170

January . . . Brittany
February 2 . . Séez
„ [c. 25] Caen
March 3 . . . Portsmouth
April 5 . . . Windsor
„ [c. 10] . London
June 11 . . . London
„ 14, 15 . . Westminster
„ [c. 24] . . Portsmouth
Barfleur
„ [c. 30] . . Falaise
[July] . . . . Argentan
July 6 . . . . La Ferté Bernard
„ 20, 22 . . Vendome near Fréteval
August . . . La Mote Garnier, near Damfront
September . . Roque Madour
October . . . Tours
„ 12 . . Amboise
Chaumont
Chinon
[November] . . Loches

1170 (*continued*)

November 23 . Mont Luçon
    „   26 . Bourges
December 21 . Bayeux
    „   25 . Bur-le-Roi
    „   31 . Argentan

1171

January 1–
February [c.
    10] . . . . Argentan
February [c. 11– Pont Orson
    25] . . . .
[March, April] . [Brittany]
May 2–16   . . Pont Orson
[June, July] . Normandy
         Valognes
August 2 . . . Portsmouth
    „   [c. 5] . Winchester
September [c. 8] Welsh border
    „   25 . Pembroke
    „   27 . St. David's
    „   29– .
October 15   Pembroke
    „   16 . . Milford Haven
    „   17–31 . Waterford
November 6   . Cashel
    „   11–
December 31 . Dublin

1172

January,
February . . Dublin
March, April
    1–16 . . . Wexford
April 17 . . . Portfinnan
    „   [19] . . Haverfordwest
    „   21 . . . Pembroke
    „   22 . . . Cardiff

April 23 . . . Newport
    „   24 . . . Talacharn
May [c. 12] . . Portsmouth
         Barfleur
    „   16 . . . Gorram, in
         Maine
    „   17 . . . Savigny
    „   21 . . . Avranches
[June–August] . Brittany
September
    [c. 29] . . . Caen
[December] . . Le Mans
    „   25–31 Chinon

1173

[January] . . Montferrand,
         in Auvergne
February 21–28 Limoges
March [c. 1] . . Vigeois
    „   5 . . Chinon
    „   7 . . Alençon
    „   [c. 10] . Gisors
April 4 . . . St. Barbe
    „   8 . . . Alençon
April–June . Rouen
[June, c. 25] . Northampton
July . . . . Rouen
August 6, 7 . . Conches
    „   8 . . . Bréteuil,
         Conches
    „   9 . . . Verneuil
    „   10 . . . Damville
    „   [c. 12–20] . Rouen
    „   22–29 . Dol
September 8–15 Le Mans
    „   25, 26 Gisors
[November] . . Anjou
November 30 . Vendome
December 25 . Caen

1174

January–April	. Normandy
April 30 . . .	. Le Mans
May 12 . . .	. Poitiers
[May]	. Saintes
June 11 . . .	. Ancenis
„ 24 . . .	. Bonneville
July 7 . . .	. Barfleur
„ 8 . . .	. Southampton
„ 12, 13 . .	. Canterbury
„ 14–17 . .	. Westminster
„ 20, 21 . .	. Huntingdon
„ 24, 25 . .	. Seleham
„ [27] . .	. Brampton
„ 31 . . .	. Northampton
August 8 . . .	. Portsmouth
	Barfleur
„ 11–14 . .	. Rouen
September 8 .	. Gisors
„ c. 22 .	. Poitiers
„ 30 .	. Mont Louis, near Tours
[October] . . .	. Falaise
December [c. 1]	Falaise
„ 8 .	. Valognes
„ 25 .	. Argentan

1175

January . . .	. Anjou
February 2 . .	. Le Mans
„ 24 . .	. Gisors
„ 26 . .	. Rouen
March	. Anjou
„ 25 . . .	. Caen
April 1 . . .	. Bur-le-Roi
„ [c. 3] . .	. Valognes
„ 13 . .	. Cherbourg
„ 22 . .	. Caen

May 8	. Barfleur
„ 9	. Portsmouth
„ 18	. Westminster
„ 28	. Canterbury
June 1 . . .	. Reading
[June]	. Woodstock
June 24 . . .	. Oxford
„ 29 . . .	. Gloucester
July 1–8 . . .	. Woodstock
„ 9 . . .	. Lichfield
August 1 . . .	. Nottingham
„ 10 . . .	. York
[September] . .	. [Stamford]
	[Northampton]
	London
	Windsor
October 8 . .	. Windsor
„ 31 . .	. Winchester
November . .	. Windsor
„ 26 .	. Eynsham
„ c. 30 .	. Winchester
December 25–31	Windsor

1176

January 26 . .	. Northampton
March 14 . .	. London
April 4 . . .	. Winchester
May 25 . . .	. Westminster
„ [c. 30] . .	. Winchester
[June–August] .	. Clarendon
	Ludgershall
	Titgrave
	Marlborough
	Geddington
	Nottingham
	Feckenham
	Bridgnorth
	[Shrewsbury]
August 15 . .	. Winchester

1176 (*continued*)

September 21 . Winchester
   ,,   28 . Windsor
October, c. 9 . Feckenham
   ,,   17 . Cirencester
November 12 . Westminster
December 24, 25 Nottingham

1177

January, c. 15 . Northampton
   ,,   20 . Windsor
February 2 . . Marlborough
   ,,   22 . . Winchester
March 9 . . . Windsor
   ,,   13 . . . Westminster
   ,, [c. 20] . . Marlborough
April 17 . . . Reading
   ,,   21 . . . Canterbury
   ,,   22 . . . Dover
   ,,   23, 24 . Wye
   ,,   c. 26 . London
May 1 . . . . Bury St. Ed-
               munds
   ,,   2 . . . . Ely
May . . . . Geddington
               Windsor
               Oxford
   ,, 22 . . . . Amesbury
   ,, 29 . . . . Winchester
June [c. 10] . . London
   ,,   11 . . Waltham
   ,,   12 . . London
       c. 16 . . Woodstock
July 1 . . . . Winchester
   ,,   9 . . . . Stokes, near
               Portsmouth
   ,, 10–17 . . Stanstead, in
               Westbourne

July c. 17–
   August 15 . Winchester
August 18 . . Portsmouth
   ,,   19 . . Caplevic
September [c. 1] Ivry
   ,,   11 . Rouen
   ,,   21 . Near Ivry
   ,,   25 . Nonancourt
[October] . . . Verneuil
             Alençon
             Argentan
             Berri
   ,,   9 . . Châteauroux
             La Châtre
             Limousin
             Berri
[November] . . Graszay
             Grammont
December 25. Angers

1178

March 19 . . . Bec-Hellouin
April 9 . . . Angers
July 15 . . . "Dighesmut,"
             on English
             coast
[July] . . . . Canterbury
             London
August 6 . . . Woodstock
December 25 . Winchester

1179

[January–
   March] . . . Winchester
             Windsor
             Gloucester
April 1 . . . Winchester
   ,,   10 . . . Windsor

August 23 . . Dover
    Canterbury
 ,, 26 . . Dover
 ,, 27 . . Westminster
[October] . . . Windsor
    Worcester
December 25 . Nottingham

1180

[January] . . Oxford
[April] . . . Reading
April [15] . . Portsmouth
    Alençon
 ,, 20 . . . Le Mans
[May] . . . . Chinon
June 28 . . . Gisors
[July–
 September] Quillebœuf
    Bonneville
    Argentan
    Caen
    Bur-le-Roy
    Valognes
    Cherbourg
    Tenchebray
    Damfront
    Mortain
    Gorron
    Lions-la-Forêt
    Driencourt
    Falaise
September c. 29 Gisors
December 25 . Le Mans
   c. 31 . Angers

1181

[March] . . . [Ivry]
    Grammont
March 5 . . . Valasse
April 5 . . . Chinon

April 27 . . . near Nonan-
    court
[May] . . . . Barfleur
[July] . . . . Gisors
July 26 . . . Cherbourg
    Portsmouth
[August] . . . Canterbury
    Nottingham
    Pontefract
    York
    Knaresborough
    Richmond
    Lichfield
    Feckenham
September 6 . . Evesham
 ,, 12 . Winchester
December 25 . Winchester

1182

January 6 . . Marlborough
[February] . . [Arundel]
February 21, 22 Bishops Wal-
    tham
March, c. 10 . . Portsmouth
    Barfleur
[March–May] . Senlis
    Poitou
    Grammont
    St. Yriez
    Pierre Buffière
June 24 . . . Grammont
July 1 . . . . Perigueux
 ,, c. 6 . . . Limoges
December 25 . Caen

1183

January 1 . . Le Mans
[February] . . Limoges
    Aixe

1183 (*continued*)

March 1 . . . Limoges
" 8 . . . Poitiers
March . . . . Angers
Mirebeau
April 17–
June 24 . . . Limoges
Le Mans
July 3 . . . . Angers
December 6 . . Gisors
" 25 . Le Mans

1184

[January–May] Limoges
Evreux
Rouen
June, c. 5 . . Choisi
" 10 . . . Wissant
Dover
" c. 12 . . Canterbury
" c. 13 . . London
July 22 . . . Worcester
" c. 25 . . Winchester
August 5 . . . Reading
" 16 . . Woodstock
" c. 21 . Dover
Canterbury
London
October 21–23 . Windsor
December 1–13 . Westminster
" 14 . Canterbury
" 15, 16 London
" 25 . Windsor
" c. 31 . Guildford

1185

January 1-6 . . Winchester
" 25 . . Melkesham

[February] . . Chipping
Campden
March [c. 10] . Nottingham
" 17 . . . Reading
" 18 . . . Clerkenwell
Westminster
" 31 . . . Windsor
April 10–16 . . Dover
" 16 . . . Wissant
" 21 . . Rouen
May 1 . . . . Vaudreuil
November 7 . . Aumâle
" 9 . . Belvoir
December 25 . Damfront

1186

[February] . . Gisors
March 10, 11 . Gisors
April 27 . . . Southampton
" c. 30 . . Merewell
Winchester
May 25 . . Eynsham
Oxford
July 1 . . . . Northampton
" 15 . . . Feckenham
[July] . . . . Carlisle
September 5 . . Woodstock
" 9–14 Marlborough
October 20 . . Reading
November 30 . Amesbury
December 25, 26 Guildford

1187

January 1 . . Westminster
February 10 . . Chilham
" 11 . Canterbury
" 14–17 Dover
" 17 . Wissant

February 18	. Hesdin
„ 19	. Driencourt
„ c. 20	. Aumâle
April 5 . .	. Gué St. Remy,
	near Nonan-
	court
June 23 . .	. Châteauroux
August 28 .	. Alençon
[September].	. Angers
	Brittany
	Montreleis
[November] .	. Bur-le-Roy
December 25	. Caen

1188

January c. 4	. Barfleur
„ 13-21	. Gisors
„ 23 .	. Le Mans
„ c. 25	. Alençon
„ 29 .	. Dieppe
„ 30 .	. Winchelsea
[February] .	. Oxford
	Northampton
„ 11	. Geddington
	Bury St.
	Edmunds
„ 29—
March 1 . .	. Clarendon
	[Cirencester]
[March-April]	. Kingston-on-
	Thames

[March-April]	. Winchester
	Woodstock
June 5 . .	. London
„ 14 . .	. Geddington
July 10 . .	. Portsea
„ 11 . .	. Barfleur
„ [12] . .	. Alençon
„ 16-18 .	. Gisors
„ 30 . .	. Mantes
September .	. Ivry
October [c. 1]	. [Gisors]
„ 7 .	. Châtillon
November 18	. Bonmoulins
December .	. Guienne
„ 25	. Saumur

1189

February 1-3	. Le Mans
March 20 .	. Le Mans
May 19 . .	. Le Mans
June 4-9 . .	. La Ferté
	Bernard
„ 10-12 .	. Le Mans
„ 12 . .	. Frenelles
„ 18 . .	. Savigny
July 3 . .	. Azay
„ 4 . .	. Colombier
„ 5, 6 . .	. Chinon : death
	of King
	Henry

INDEX

R